Alexander Garvin

Parks, Recreation, and Open Space: A Twenty-First Century Agenda

ALEXANDER GARVIN

John Singer Sargent

Foreword

This Planning Advisory Service Report is sponsored, in part, by the City Parks Forum. CPF is a fellowship of mayors, their park advisors, and community leaders that encourages collaboration, the sharing of information, and an exchange of ideas about the role of parks in communites. The American Planning Association administers the CPF program, which is made possible by support from the Wallace-Reader's Digest Funds and the Doris Duke Charitable Foundation. For more information about CPF, the forums already held, the mayors who have attended, and the parks programs that have benefitted from CPF grants, go to APA's web site (www.planning.org), e-mail CPF at cpf@planning.org, or call 312-431-9100.

APA developed CPF to reach out to mayors to persuade and encourage them to elevate the status of parks on their agendas and in their city's budget. CPF staff consulted with a number of parks advocates from around the country about the structure and content of the program. One of the issues that these advocates prominently mentioned was the need for a better explanation for mayors of what parks have been, what parks are, and what parks will need to be to be successful in the "new" economics and society of twenty-first century America. This topic was, in many ways, at the heart of the program. Without a common understanding of what we meant when we used the word "parks" and a solid understanding of the history of park development in the United States, how could we communicate effectively with CPF participants and all the others who were interested in this program?

With that thought in mind, we commissioned Alexander Garvin to write this report. We were very fortunate that Alex had the time to undertake this task. As a commissioner on the New York City Planning Commission, an Adjunct Professor of Urban Planning and Management at Yale University, a private consultant, and the planning director for NYC2012, the committee to bring the Summer Olympics to New York in 2012, he is very much in demand. We knew he had the intelligence, the talent, and the enthusiasm for the task because those qualities were clearly evident in his book, *The American City: What Works, What Doesn't* (McGraw-Hill, 1995), winner of the 1996 American Institute of Architects book award in urbanism, and *Urban Parks and Open Space* (the Trust for Public Land and the Urban Land Institute, 1997), of which he was a principal author.

I asked Alex to reflect on the core issue that park advocates had presented us; namely, what should be the agenda for parks in the U.S. in the early twenty-first century if they are to be recognized as an essential cornerstone of any great community? To develop such an agenda, Alex has chosen first to describe the parks agenda developed by Frederick Law Olmsted, which dominated the design of American parks from their beginnings in the middle of the nineteenth century to the middle of the twentieth century. Alex notes, however, that Olmsted's agenda has been surpassed by the societal changes brought about by the suburbanization of the U.S. and its effect on the way people think of parks, recreation, and open space. And there have also been changes in the role of government as a supplier of these essentials, which, as Alex points out, have regrettably too often been misunderstood and treated as amenities or luxuries.

The agenda offered in this report addresses park, recreation, and open space acquisition, financing, creation, development, and maintenance in the new century. It is solidly founded on those efforts and places that have succeeded in creating successful parks and related spaces in the latter half of the twentieth century. (It needs to be noted here that Alex has included only case studies and photos of places he has been; his stunning photography, along with his written analysis, testify to the beauty and success of many of these spaces.)

Using his first-hand knowledge of these places, he has distilled a set of principles from the case studies. From those principles, he has developed a clear set of actions to guide public and private leaders in all aspects of park, recreation, and open space development. As all good educators do, he has (1) built an argument for his agenda by documenting the best of what has come before and what made it best; (2) acknowledged that, in the current environment, we cannot recreate the past (nor should we try—it was, after all, a different time, place, and circumstance); and (3) moved on to challenge community leaders to push themselves to build new ideas from the models he has provided—ideas that will fit these times and circumstances.

Some of what Alex writes in this report may upset people. That's good. Without challenge, thought is stagnant. Thoughtful and insightful challenges tear apart that "box" that everyone is talking about when they say that we need to learn to think "outside the box." So, we at PAS and CPF hope you'll accept Alex's challenge and get outside your box. Consider his agenda. Parks are too important to the fabric of our communities and our lives to not spend more time and effort revolving in our minds the questions that he raises and the suggestions that he offers.

Are there answers in this report to the questions our parks advocates posed? It depends. While I think we have found that there is no universal answer to the question, What is a park?, you may find that some of what is offered in this report is testament to what a park can and should be, especially in your community to meet the needs of the people there. The rest is up to you.

Jim Hecimovich
Chief Editor, PAS Reports

Alexander Garvin

Frederick Law Olmsted set forth an ambitious agenda to provide every American with access to public open space.

PART 1

The Olmsted Agenda

D uring the second half of the nineteenth century, Frederick Law Olmsted set forth an ambitious agenda to provide every American with access to public open space. That agenda included public acquisition of huge amounts of land for public parks, parkways, playgrounds, nature preserves, and integrated regional park systems. For developing suburban areas, he advocated setting houses back from tree-lined streets on open landscaped lots. The trees gave the houses a modicum of privacy and provided the streets and sidewalks with shade and a more natural appearance, thereby making these public spaces more pleasant for people walking or riding by.

Olmsted was neither the first nor the only advocate for this open space agenda. A large, effective coalition of supporters came together to press for the creation of public parks. It began with nineteenth century reformers who believed that parks acted as an antidote to the "evils" of urbanization (Fein 1968). They were joined by property owners who saw parks as a means of increasing the value of their holdings, politicians who thought of them as an opportunity to provide jobs and patronage, and community groups that believed parks would improve neighborhoods. During the twentieth century, environmentalists who demanded that parks offer sustainable habitats for a wide range of flora and fauna joined the coalition.

Alexander Garvin

Central Park, New York City. Olmsted intended parks to provide a means of escape "from the cramped, confined and controlling circumstances of the streets of the town, in other words, *a sense of enlarged freedom* " (Beveridge and Hoffman 1997, 83)

"Dens of Death," Baxter St., New York City, 1901. Nineteenth century reformers thought parks were an antidote to such "evils" of urbanization as the wooden shanties on Baxter Street on New York City's lower East Side.

Jacob Riss

TABLE 1. 10 LARGE CITIES WITH THE HIGHEST PARK ACREAGE
(Land Held by County, State, and City Park Agencies Within City Boundaries)

City	1990 Population	Total Acreage
New York City	7,381,000	52,938
Phoenix	1,159,000	36,501
San Diego	1,171,000	36,108
Los Angeles	3,554,000	30,121
Dallas	1,053,000	21,828
Houston	1,744,000	21,790
Kansas City, Missouri	441,000	13,329
Indianapolis	747,000	13,239
Portland, Oregon	481,000	12,591
Chicago	2,722,000	11,629

Source: Harnik (2000).

The open space agenda this coalition advocated has been achieved. In 2001, any American who wants to go to a public park has a vast array of choices. The National Park Service manages 80.7 million acres (www.nps.gov). City governments administer even more open space. There are 52,938 acres of parkland in New York City, 36,501 acres in Phoenix, and 36,108 acres in San Diego (Harnik 2000, 121). In addition to individual public parks and integrated regional park systems, the country also has the benefit of a myriad of parkways, playgrounds, and nature preserves. In most suburbs, residents enjoy the green relief provided by the private yards and tree-lined streets that Olmsted prescribed.

Because of this remarkable achievement, public officials assume erroneously that we can divert resources to other "more pressing" needs. Yet, demand for open space has not abated. The need to satisfy this demand has led public officials to shift some of the burden of supplying open space to the private sector. The results of this shift have not been uniformly successful. It is time to alter the regulatory environment in a manner that will encourage property owners to create better, more usable open space.

Despite the vast inventory of public open space, government is no longer the primary supplier of recreation resources. Too much of its inventory is in the wrong place, or does not include attractive facilities, or has slid into a shameful state of disrepair, or is not available for public use. More and more frequently, America's increasingly diverse, mobile, and affluent population chooses to spend its leisure time and money on an extraordinary array of alternatives.

The success stories in this report are important exceptions that demonstrate the important role that government should play in its stewardship of the public realm. Taken together, these successes constitute an agenda for the twenty-first century that calls on public agencies to:

- update public facilities in response to continually changing public demand;
- manage the public realm efficiently and economically;
- renovate and reposition publicly owned property for public use;
- reclaim abandoned property for public use;
- combine recreation with other functions; and
- make more effective use of open space in public projects.

TABLE 2. 10 LARGE CITIES WITH THE HIGHEST PERCENTAGE OF OPEN SPACE
(Land Held by County, State, and City Park Agencies Within City Boundaries)

City	Area of City	Open Space(%)
New York City	197,696 Acres	52,938 Acres (26.8%)
San Francisco	29,888 Acres	7,594 Acres (25.4%)
San Diego	207,360 Acres	36,108 Acres (17.4%)
Portland, Oregon	79,808 Acres	12,591 Acres (15.8%)
Boston	30,976 Acres	4,865 Acres (15.7%)
Cincinnati	49,408 Acres	7,391 Acres (15.0%)
Phoenix	268,736 Acres	36,501 Acres (13.6%)
Philadelphia	86,464 Acres	10,685 Acres (12.4%)
Seattle	53,696 Acres	6,194 Acres (11.5%)
Los Angeles	300,351 Acres	30,121 Acres (10.0%)

Average of 25 Largest Cities: 11.0%

Source: Harnik (2000).

FREDERICK LAW OLMSTED

John Singer Sargent

Frederick Law Olmsted was born in 1822 in Hartford, Connecticut, and died in 1903 in Waverly, Massachusetts. He had trouble finding a suitable career. After working for a dry goods company in New York City and sitting in on some of his brother's classes at Yale, the spirit of adventure led him at the age of 21 to become an apprentice sailor on a square-rigged sailing ship bound for Canton, China.

When he returned from the Orient, Olmsted tried farming, first in Connecticut and then on Staten Island. He was not well suited to farming, either. Next, he tried jour-

nalism. The stories he filed during a trip to England were followed with a more daring adventure to the ante-bellum South that resulted in a series of articles that provide significant information on daily life in the pre-Civil War South. These articles were compiled into books that are still in print and read by tens of thousands of Americans who have no idea that their author rejected journalism, just as he had rejected farming.

Olmsted's writings were sufficiently popular for him to enter the publishing business. Unfortunately, his foray into publishing only increased his debts. In need of a way to support himself, in 1857 he accepted a position as superintendent of the site selected for New York City's proposed Central Park. An acquaintance, architect Calvert Vaux, suggested they join forces and enter the design competition for the new park. Their plan was the winner among the 33 submissions. Thus began their partnership, which lasted till 1861, when Olmsted became Secretary of the United States Sanitary Commission, responsible for taking care of wounded Civil War Soldiers. After two years, he moved to California to become director of the Mariposa Mining Company. When that venture failed,

Vaux convinced him to resume their partnership. It lasted till 1872, when Olmsted founded his own firm.

During the next 23 years, Olmsted designed landscape settings for private estates, public institutions (including the U.S. Capitol), cemeteries, parks, parkways, playgrounds, and suburban subdivisions. These were not mere decorative plantings. Many of them established national standards. For example, while designing the grounds for the Biltmore Estate in Asheville, North Carolina, Olmsted pioneered the nation's first effort at scientific forest management.

At one time or another, Olmsted's partners included Calvert Vaux, Henry Codman, Charles Eliot, and most notably his stepson/nephew John Charles Olmsted (in 1859 he married his brother's widow, Mary Perkins Olmsted) and his natural-born son Frederick Law Olmsted Jr. By 1950, when Frederick Law Olmsted Jr. closed the firm, it had been involved in 5,500 projects, including 650 parks and recreation areas, 900 private estates, and 270 subdivisions and planned communities.

Sources: National Association for Olmsted Parks (1987); Rybczynski (1999).

State St., Chicago, 1869. During the second part of the nineteenth century, most city streets, even in populous cities like Chicago, were noisy, unpaved thoroughfares in which pedestrians were forced to jostle with horses, carts, and delivery vehicles. The residents and workers in the buildings that lined these streets were eager to find places to which to escape, even if it was for just an hour or two.

The public realm to which city dwellers might escape consisted of unpaved streets, squares, marketplaces, or vast tracts of wilderness outside the city.

CITIES AND SUBURBS IN 1850

Twenty-three million people lived in the United States in 1850, of which about 3.5 million or 15 percent lived in cities. Only seven cities had populations more than 100,000. New York was the largest, with 516,000 inhabitants, not counting the independent city of Brooklyn, which, with a population of 139, 000, ranked third. Historians estimate that most people worked more than 60 hours per week, with only Sundays free. The average family consisted of 5.5 persons who lived in small, cramped dwellings.

City dwellers, who spent most of their waking hours at physically demanding jobs, had few opportunities to occupy what little leisure time they had. Organized sports were not common, though baseball and an early form of football were popular, and rowing was a social attraction in cities with protected rivers. Those with enough money went to the theater and to concerts, or bet on sports like horse racing (in the North) or cock fighting (in the South and West), or spent an evening at a beer garden.

The public realm to which city dwellers might escape consisted of unpaved streets, squares, marketplaces, or vast tracts of wilderness outside the city. In every American city, whether traveling by foot, on horseback or in a carriage, the public was confronted with noisy, littered, unpaved thoroughfares. As unkempt as they were, city streets, squares, greens, and marketplaces served an important civic function. They provided large numbers of people with some open space and a limited amount of physical and psychological relief from their small, overcrowded living quarters. They did not provide much room, however, for active sports and none of the "sense of enlarged freedom" that was later to be had in public parks.

City governments did not spend much on the upkeep of these places. Municipal spending for infrastructure and public facilities concentrated on water supply, drainage, and buildings that housed the city administration, the courts, and the police. There were as yet no parks created specifically for public recreation, no public gymnasiums, and no public libraries. School boards operated new fee-paying public schools. But most civic agencies, such as boards of health, were temporary bodies with a small emergency staff. Their organization was often loose and relied on volunteer services (e.g., fire fighting). Private companies operated other services, such as gaslighting.

As more and more people squeezed into already crowded areas, reformers demanded public action to relieve congestion. The absence of public parks was becoming an election issue in cities across the country. Political bosses and ordinary laborers saw parks as opportunities for patronage and jobs. Property owners saw them as opportunities to profit from their real estate investments.

When Ambrose Kingsland ran for Mayor of New York City in 1850, he sought the support of all these constituencies. After the election, he introduced legislation calling for the park he had promised and set forth the public policy rationale for its creation. In a message to the Common Council in 1851, he explained that people "would rejoice in being able to breathe pure air in such a place, while they ride and drive through its avenues free from . . . noise, dust, and confusion." That place, now known as Central Park, would become America's first major public park.

OLMSTED'S NINETEENTH CENTURY AGENDA

There may have been a constituency for expansion of the public realm, but there was as yet no publicly accepted agenda when Frederick Law Olmsted came on the scene. Over the next half century, he gave form to an agenda that included public parks, playgrounds, boulevards and parkways, park systems, conservation, and suburban subdivisions.

Public Parks

Today, Olmsted is thought of as America's premier landscape architect. But in 1857, when at the age of 35 he was hired to be the first superintendent of the site acquired for New York's Central Park, Olmsted was a

Central Park, New York City, 1992. Olmsted believed that parks would improve physical health by supplying "air screened and purified by trees, and recently acted upon by sunlight." He also believed that they would improve mental health by providing an "opportunity to escape from conditions requiring vigilance, wariness, and activity toward other(s)." (Beveridge and Hoffman 1997, 182)

Alexander Garvin

failed farmer and sometime journalist. As superintendent he came to know the territory set aside for the park and saw opportunities others had missed. Together with Calvert Vaux, he devised the scheme, which won a competition for the park's design.

That scheme achieved four objectives:

1) Providing "green relief" from the noise and confusion of the city

2) Opening up places for "play"

3) Creating a common space where diverse populations could intermingle

4) Investing public monies in a way that would have a significant payoff in shaping the land and creating real estate opportunities.

Although at the time public parks were virtually unheard of, the first two objectives were widely accepted. The most important of these two was to provide an idyllic counterpoint to the noise and confusion of the city—a place where green pastures and still waters could restore the soul. To achieve the second, the park included places where residents, especially children, could play, thereby relieving the tensions of urban life.

Central Park's third objective was more ambitious. Its designers conceived of the park as a melting pot for the city's heterogeneous population. It did not take long for this objective to be achieved. Writing in 1870, Olmsted explained that Central Park had become a place where "vast numbers of persons [were] brought closely together, poor and rich, young and old . . . each individual adding by his mere presence to the pleasure of all others" (Sutton 1971, 75). Two years later he described a typical Sunday, during which more than 70,000 entered the park. "A large number were taken in omnibuses—special park vehicles carrying ten or twelve each—and most of them must have traveled at least three miles to reach the lower end of the park" (Schuyler and Censer 1992, 551).

The most significant objective of public investment in parks, however, was its strategic value in encouraging real estate development in the blocks surrounding the park, altering land-use patterns and reshaping the very character of city life. When the site was acquired, most city residents lived more than three miles to the south. In many places public streets mapped for the largely undeveloped surrounding territory, remained to be installed. Within a decade and a half, the value of property in the wards surrounding Central Park had increased nine times. Citywide values, during that period, had only doubled (Fox 1990). The real estate taxes generated from this increase in value were enough "to pay the entire principal and interest of the cost of the park in less time than was required for its construction" (Cleveland 1883). Cities everywhere wanted to outperform New York. Within a few years similar parks were being created in many other cities.

The most important of these two objectives was to provide an idyllic counterpoint to the noise and confusion of the city—a place where green pastures and still waters could restore the soul.

CALVERT VAUX

When Calvert Vaux joined Olmsted to work on Central Park, he was a British-born, 33-year old architect who had migrated to America six years earlier. Olmsted and Vaux maintained their partnership for five years until Olmsted left to become Secretary of the United States Sanitary Commission. They resumed their partnership in 1866 and formally terminated it as of 1872, although from time to time they joined forces to work on other projects. Working with a variety of partners, Vaux prepared designs for parks, gardens, private residences, and public buildings, most notably New York's Metropolitan Museum of Art and the American Museum of Natural History. Like Olmsted, he was a prolific writer of magazine and newspaper articles and park reports. His most important book, Villas and Cottages, published in 1857, includes numerous drawings of houses and their floor plans. He died in Brookly in 1895.

Source: William Alex and George B. Tatum, Calvert Vaux: Architect and Planner (New York: Ink, Inc., 1994)

Alexander Garvin

Central Park, 1998. Olmsted designed Central Park to be a place that would bring together huge numbers of people of every age, income, class, and ethnicity.

Alexander Garvin

Washington Park, Chicago, 1997. Washington Park was the first public park designed to include spaces for active sports like football and baseball.

Play Areas

When Olmsted and Vaux designed Washington Park for Chicago's South Park Commission in 1870, they included playing fields for organized sports for the first time in a public park. Olmsted did not invent the public playground. At that time, there was neither an agreed-upon agenda for the creation of playgrounds nor a generally accepted conception of what a playground ought to be. Twenty years later, however, Olmsted did help to define its contents and appearance. In designing the 10-acre site in Boston that became Charlesbank, Olmsted engaged Professor Dudley Sargent of Harvard to design play equipment. Today, slides, swings, and sandboxes can be found in playgrounds across America.

Charlesbank Park, Boston, 1892. Charlesbank Park (demolished to make way for Massachusetts General Hospital) provided public recreation areas with some of the country's earliest professionally designed playground equipment.

Avenue Foch, Paris, 1998. Georges-Eugene Haussmann conceived of Avenue Foch as a grand residential boulevard linking the Arc de Triomphe with the new public park being created out of the Bois de Boulogne. It was originally known as Avenue de l'Emperatrice in honor of Napoleon III's wife.

Alexander Garvin

Alexander Garvin

Eastern Parkway, Brooklyn, 2000. Olmsted & Vaux were inspired by the Avenue Foch to create a parkway where residents could walk, ride or drive in a parklike setting on their way to the new Prospect Park.

Parkways

Mid-nineteenth century cities often included tree-lined streets. Landscaped boulevards and parkways, however, were unknown. Inspired by Avenue Foch, in Paris, Olmsted proposed landscaped parkways for Brooklyn, Chicago, Buffalo, and Boston. They were not simple roadways. Olmsted's parkways were linear extensions of parks and, thus, in his words: places where "driving, riding, and walking can be conveniently pursued in association with pleasant people, and without the liability of encountering the unpleasant sights . . . [of] the common streets" (Fein 1968, 157). Living opposite a parkway was more desirable than living on a narrow street. Consequently, parkway properties tended to be developed more rapidly than more distant sites and were usually occupied by more expensive buildings. Cities as diverse as Albany and Denver took Olmsted's advice and created parkways as a way of providing character and focus to developing neighborhoods.

Alexander Garvin

Chapin Parkway, Buffalo, New York, 1991. Olmsted & Vaux's Buffalo parkways provided choice locations for residential construction.

Fenway, Boston, 1999. Olmsted's scheme for the Fenway section of the Emerald Necklace converted a pestilent swamp into a recreation facility that became a desirable location for new real estate development.

Emerald Necklace Plan, Boston. Olmsted designed a park system that exploited the "peculiar excellence" of specific sites, which, when combined, provided the widest range of parks, play areas, and parkways for a user population from both Boston and Brookline.

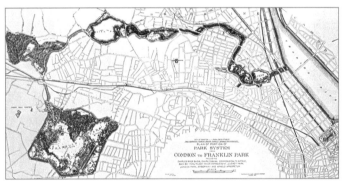

Courtesy of the National Park Service, Frederick Law Olmsted National Historic Site

Integrated Park Systems

While Olmsted understood that parks, parkways, and playgrounds served the residents of surrounding neighborhoods, he thought they should be planned as integrated systems so that the components could function in conjunction with one another. Consequently, he recommended creating facilities that would exploit the "peculiar excellence" of each specific site. Taken separately, they might not be nearest to the people seeking their use. But, taken together, these different parks, play areas, and parkways would provide the wide range of recreation opportunities desired by a large, complex urban population (Sutton 1971, 236). Voters in Louisville, Minneapolis, Seattle, and many other cities agreed. They adopted this agenda and began developing such park systems.

Franklin Park, Boston, 1994. The open meadow Olmsted created in the Franklin Park section of the Emerald Necklace quickly became a popular site for golf.

Natural Areas

Although often overlooked, Olmsted was one of the nation's earliest conservationists. In 1864, when he had moved to northern California to become superintendent of the Mariposa Mining Estate, President Lincoln signed a bill deeding the land we know today as Yosemite National Park to the State of California. Three months later, Governor Frederick Low appointed Olmsted chairman of a commission to decide on the future of this extraordinary place. After supervising a survey of the site, he wrote a report recommending the creation of approach roads and an internal circulation system that would simultaneously forever protect the landscape and open it to thousands of tourists. As he explained: "It is but sixteen years since the Yosemite was first seen by a white man. . . . If proper facilities are offered . . . in a century the number of visitors will be counted in millions" (Ranney 1990, 507). How right he was. In 1999 more than 3.6 million people visited Yosemite (www.nps.gov).

Olmsted believed that nature preserves had to be more than wilderness protected from human incursion. Natural areas, he felt, could be protected and also made available for the enjoyment of large numbers of people by introducing into the landscape pedestrian paths, vehicular roadways, scenic overlooks, camp sites, and lodging and maintenance structures that would direct the flow of crowds in an appropriate manner. Otherwise, as he explained in 1887 when he was working on the preservation of Niagara Falls, how could it be protected from visitors who were likely to be "unconscious of wrong purposes and indignant at obvious constraints upon what [they regard] as harmless conduct" (Olmsted 1887).

Suburban Development

For newly developing suburbs, Olmsted recommended a different settlement pattern. He argued that, in addition to community interaction in parks, playgrounds, landscaped boulevards, and nature preserves, there had to be room around every house for "constant intercourse, and interdependence between families" (Schuyler and Censer 1992, 287). His first foray into suburban subdivision design came in 1868-69, for Riverside, Illinois. Olmsted's plan established minimum lot sizes of 100 feet by 225 feet. Houses had to be set back 30 feet from the property line. Stables and carriage houses (later used as garages) had to be located at the back of the property. Fences and hedges were not permitted at the front of the lot. Two trees along the property line provided the only privacy from people walking or driving by. Consequently, the public realm extended visually beyond streets and sidewalks, onto private property.

Houses on large lots with front, rear, and side yards became a model for suburban development. Olmsted did not invent it. But, at Riverside, he did demonstrate how it could be used in combination with curvilinear roads to transform flat, undifferentiated landscapes into handsome, Arcadian living environments. When his firm used this formula in more complex topographical situations (like that of Brookline Hill in suburban Boston or Indian Hills in suburban Louisville), it became a mechanism to exploit the advantages of the site. In such situations roadways were located at the bottom of valleys, along ledges, or at the tops of hills and ridges. This provided safe travel, easy drainage, and often wonderful views from the upper floors of houses that overlooked the roofs of those below.

Yosemite National Park, California, 1995.
Olmsted's recommendations for Yosemite preserved one of the natural wonders of the world, while simultaneously introducing the roads that made it accessible to millions of visitors.

Louisville, Kentucky, 1996. At Indian Hills (1925-1926), the Olmsted firm located roads at the bottom of valleys, along ledges, or at the tops of hills and ridges in order to provide safe travel, easy drainage, and often wonderful views.

Cottsold Road, Brookline, Massachusetts, 1999. The roads at Brookline Hill (1884) are adjusted to the topography in a manner that both minimizes the slope and provides good views over the roofs of houses located along those roads.

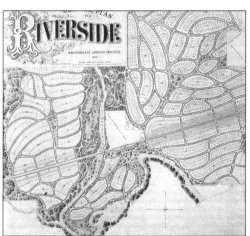

Riverside Plan, Riverside, Illinois, 1869. By providing open front lawns and attractive winding roads that encouraged "constant intercourse and interdependence between families" (Schuyler and Censer 1992, 287), the plan for Riverside became a paradigm for open space planning in suburban subdivisions.

Curving road with trees, Sudbrook, Maryland, 1997. By siting houses on open lawns set back from the street and then planting trees at the property line, Olmsted's design of Sudbrook (1889) provided what he believed was the necessary combination of community and privacy.

By 1950, America was a radically different place from the one in which a century earlier Olmsted had begun setting forth an agenda for parks, recreation, and open space.

CITIES AND SUBURBS IN 1950

By 1950, America was a radically different place from the one in which a century earlier Olmsted had begun setting forth an agenda for parks, recreation, and open space. Successive waves of immigration and a baby boom had swelled the population to 150 million, of which two-thirds lived in cities. New York, with a population of 7.9 million, was still the nation's largest city, though it was one among 66 cities with populations greater than 100,000.

Rather than being located at the center of an agricultural hinterland or the edge of undeveloped territory, most cities were now at the center of large territories rapidly filling up with suburban houses. Nor were they uniformly growing. In the East and Middle West, older cities were beginning a 50-year period of population decline as their residents moved to suburban homes.

A century of public investment had radically changed the public realm. Now cities had paved streets and sidewalks, water, sewer, electrical, and transit systems. Their maintenance required thousands of employees and large budgets. Local government entities also operated airports, schools, and hospitals, as well as an enormous welfare system.

Daily life for most Americans also had changed. The average American was vastly more prosperous. People now worked 45 hours per week and enjoyed a two-day weekend with substantial leisure time. The average family—which had declined in size from 5.5 to 3.5 persons—lived on $3,422. Public schooling and federal subsidies for college education meant that the population was better educated than ever before.

Living patterns also had changed. Middle-class America now lived primarily in single-family houses. About 55 percent of homes were owner-occupied, a percentage that would continue to rise. Not only did most Americans own their residence, they also owned substantial amounts of "private" open space in the form of government-mandated front, side, and rear yards, with driveways, green lawns, bushes, and trees. As driveway basketball games and backyard barbecues became increasingly common, an increasing amount of recreation, especially in suburbs, shifted from the public to the private realm.

A vast increase in recreation opportunities accompanied the increase in income and leisure time. Individual and team sports had evolved to the point that they occupied substantial amount of time across all social strata. Most Americans had developed this lifelong affection by playing school games, joining athletic leagues, sports and country clubs, and rooting for college and professional sports teams. That commitment was substantial. At football stadiums, for example, the event began at tailgating parties before the game had started. Professional sports were so important that cities with major league ball teams described themselves as being in the big leagues.

Technological advances had inaugurated an era of mass consumer consumption that greatly expanded recreation opportunities. Inexpensive radios, movies, national magazines, and paperback books all presented cheap opportunities for private escape. It was the automobile, however, that was responsible for many of the changes in the way Americans spent their recreation time. Cars reduced travel time and provided easy mobility over large distances. They enabled a growing population to commute between suburban homes and urban workplaces. The car was more than a commuting device. Driving itself had become a new form of leisure. It also provided access to new leisure opportunities in some locations (e.g., a weekend picnic in one of the newly acquired national or state parks).

I-405, Los Angeles, California, 1999. By the middle of the twentieth century, America's cities were no longer on the edge of undeveloped territory.

Hoffman Estates, Illinois, 2000. Driveway basketball games, backyard barbecues, and increasing amount of other recreational activities now take place on private property rather than in public parks.

Meadowlands, New Jersey, 2000. Tailgating before football games is one of the many forms of recreation that does not take place in public parks.

Alexander Garvin

Lake Calhoun, Minneapolis, Minnesota, 1992. The many recreational activities that take place around Lake Calhoun include bicycle riding, roller blading, jogging, volley ball, sailing, and fishing.

Minneapolis, Minnesota, Park System Map, 1943. By 1943, the Minneapolis Park System included 5,700 acres of parkland.

Source: Theodore Wirth, Minneapolis Park System 1883–1944. Minneapolis Board of Park Commissioners, 1945.

The Olmsted Agenda as of 1950

By 1950, Olmsted's agenda had become conventional wisdom. Every city included numerous parks and playgrounds. Inspired by his advocacy of park systems, many cities also supplied a vast array of recreation opportunities. The best located, best designed, and best maintained of these park systems was that of Minneapolis. By 1943 it was providing the city's 526,000 residents with 5,700 acres of parkland organized around lakes, river valleys, waterfalls, generously landscaped parkways, walking trails, bicycle paths, playgrounds and recreation centers, beaches and swimming pools, golf courses, athletic fields, picnic grounds, and flower gardens (Wirth 1944).

The conservation movement that Olmsted had spearheaded had become a national force. In 1916 Congress had created the National Parks Service to manage national parks and forests. By 1950 it administered more than 24.5 million acres of property.

The notion of landscaped parkways leading to major parks had taken a course nobody expected. Automobiles allowed drivers to travel quickly and go much farther to a far wider range of destinations. The popularity of driving began to exceed the capacity of many roads. The businesses that depended on trucking wanted to remove pleasure driving from these arterials. Park advocates clamoring for large regional facilities joined with them to demand landscaped, limited access parkways connecting regional parks. This new variety of parkway that excluded commercial traffic was safer, accommodated faster speeds along longer routes, and supplied scenic vistas. As early as the 1920s, such scenic roadways were beginning to provide access to beaches, nature preserves, and other tourist destinations. Their unanticipated impact was even more important.

Alexander Garvin

Taconic Parkway, New York,1976. Starting in 1907 with New York's Bronx River Parkway, and continuing in the 1920s and 1930s with Virginia's Colonial and Mount Vernon Parkways and Connecticut's Merritt and Wilbur Cross River Parkways, scenic highways and limited-access parkways transformed Olmsted's parkway concept into landscaped commuter arteries.

New parkland was not forthcoming at the same rate or in the same quantities as it had over the previous century.

Real estate developers understood that using these limited access parkways to drive into the city was as easy as using them to get to the country. They acquired easily accessible, cheap suburban land, subdivided it into lots, and built large quantities of affordable houses. These subdivisions, of course, reflected the design approach Olmsted had pioneered a century earlier: houses surrounded by open yards, set back from curvilinear streets.

The Post-War Agenda

With the Olmsted agenda largely implemented, local and national government spending shifted from expansion of the public realm to programs that guaranteed or redistributed income, and provided services like health, education, and welfare. New parkland was not forthcoming at the same rate or in the same quantities as it had over the previous century. While this reflected different public spending priorities, it also reflected the belief that additional parkland was no longer a major concern. City dwellers once might have needed "green relief," but now existing city park systems provided that relief. Suburbanites, ran the conventional wisdom, did not need "green relief" because they lived in bucolic settings that contained large amounts of greenery. Consequently, public spending could be directed to more pressing public needs.

The portion of Olmsted's agenda that called for private open space in developing suburban areas was universally accepted in the form of zoning and subdivision yard and setback regulations. But their adoption decreased support for the public open space component of that agenda. Because of this change in public support, park advocates no longer could depend on substantial government capital spending for large tracts of public open space. More and better public open space had to be provided in some other fashion. The easiest way was to make it the responsibility of the private sector, thereby avoiding government expenditures.

Acquiring and developing public open space and, upon completion, managing and maintaining it is expensive. Imposing this financial burden is only effective when government provides the additional money needed to cover the added expense.

The Fourteenth Amendment to the U.S. Constitution explicitly forbids states (and therefore local governments) from taking property for public use (providing open space) without compensation. But it does not preclude local governments from encouraging owners to provide public access to their property. As a result, Olmsted's agenda was expanded by having governments provide incentives to property owners (usually in the form of increased densities above zoned limits) in return for creating privately owned spaces and opening them to public use.

The rationale for public regulation of private property goes back for centuries to the very essence of our common law. Governments must have the power to establish regulations that protect the health, safety, and welfare of the community. This is implicit in the very power to govern. Thus, a zoning bonus could be used legitimately as a means for increasing open space.

Incentives are neither unconstitutional nor financial burdens. Property owners need not comply with them. Consequently, incentives cannot be considered a taking that requires government to compensate the owner.

Acquiring and developing public open space and, upon completion, managing and maintaining it is expensive. Imposing this financial burden is only effective when government provides the additional money needed to cover the added expense. There are different models for determining the amount of additional revenue that is required (Morris 2000, 11-13). But without this additional revenue, property owners would be no more likely to create and maintain public open space than revenue-starved government agencies. Developers will respond to incentives, however, only if the added cost of compliance is exceeded by the value of the benefits they obtain by complying.

This additional revenue can be obtained by allowing the property owner to build more than would otherwise be allowed. Consequently, the incentives that evolved offered a floor area bonus in exchange for providing additional open space. The form this open space had to take in order to qualify for a bonus was rarely specified and even more rarely satisfied Olmsted's demand that it be a public place in which vast numbers of persons were brought closely together.

Defining Open Space

Unfortunately, the words "open space" are not sufficiently explicit. Those words lump together three quite different territories: *private* open space, *common* open space, and *public* open space. The meaning of private open space should be obvious—space that is privately owned and probably not open to the public. But is open space *private* if it is publicly accessible? The Supreme Court has ruled that citizens have the right to public free speech (e.g., handing out leaflets and posting signs) in some privately owned spaces (e.g., shopping centers). One can ask the opposite as well. Is privately owned, privately maintained open space truly *public*? Security guards routinely eject vagrants and rowdy teenagers from shopping centers that are supposed to be open to the public and have every right to do so.

Private open space. There is a long history of mandating minimum private open space. During the nineteenth century, when millions of immigrants poured into cities, thousands died from the infectious diseases that spread easily in the poorly lit, ill-ventilated apartments into which they were crowded. Governments responded by enacting regulations requiring minimal private open space. Every habitable room had to have windows that opened onto that open space, thereby providing an equally minimal amount of light and air. The same approach to providing adequate private open space was applied to suburban development, where it was not a matter of public health. Front and side yards had to be large enough for residents to park their cars, thereby leaving room for visitors to park on the street. Rear yards had to be large enough to prevent unwarranted intrusions onto neighboring properties.

Common open space. Common open space is territory that is jointly used by a group of people. It is not public because those who do not hold it common can be excluded. It is not private either, because it has to be shared with others. In many suburban subdivisions, houses cluster around open spaces that would otherwise be divided into front or side yards. The resulting landscape is often quite pleasing—an observation that will surely be seconded by many residents who use the swimming pools, tot lots, and tennis courts that occupy this common open space.

Some common open spaces are quite generous. The golf course in a gated community is an example of such common open space. Ruby Hill, a lovely development in a 1,900-acre section of the Livermore Valley, east of San Francisco Bay, includes an 18-hole golf course designed by Jack Nicklaus, vineyards that must remain in agricultural use, and beautiful walking trails. But only the residents of this 850-unit gated community and their guests are able to enjoy this open space.

> *Common open space is not public because those who do not hold it common can be excluded.*

Alexander Garvin

Ruby Hill, Livermore Valley, California, 1999. The golf course in the gated community of Ruby Hill, is lovely common open space used by its members. But it is not a replacement for publicly owned parks that bring together large numbers of diverse people.

It is up to government to decide the form and character of the public open space that is provided.

Public open space. Public open space is territory that is owned and managed by a public agency for everybody's benefit. The enactment of zoning incentives to encourage property owners to provide open space has confused matters. Absent this effort to expand the public realm, there would be no difficulty in identifying public open space.

It is up to government to decide the form and character of the public open space that is provided. As a result of the pioneering work of Olmsted and Vaux, government agencies tend to be quite specific about the design, landscaping, and use of public parks. They also are quite specific about street and sidewalk dimensions as well as the vehicular and pedestrian traffic flows on public thoroughfares. Streets and sidewalks, however, do not exist in a vacuum. They are very much affected by the properties that surround them. Early twentieth century yard and setback requirements determined the character of what was built on those properties. Unfortunately, later twentieth century zoning incentives confused matters.

Plaza bonuses. The earliest zoning ordinances required one-family houses to set back from the property line. Such setbacks increased the amount of light and air experienced by both pedestrians and drivers moving along public thoroughfares. In 1957, Chicago became the first city to attempt to extend this approach to commercial properties. Property owners who set back their buildings a minimum of 20 feet along their entire street frontage were permitted to increase the allowable floor area within the building by 1.5 square feet for every square foot of open space (Kayden 2000, 304, n. 50). Like the setbacks for one-family houses, the bonus for open space was intended to improve the quality of contiguous streets and sidewalks. It also reflected design preferences. Modernist designers preferred buildings that were not shoehorned into crowded sites. They believed that building occupants would be healthier if they

Alexander Garvin

Plaza at 55 Monroe St., Chicago, 2000. The widened sidewalk on Chicago's Monroe Street is an example of privately owned and maintained public spaces encouraged by the city's zoning bonus.

Alexander Garvin

Seagram Plaza, New York City 1995. The plaza of the Seagram Building became the model for New York's 1961 zoning bonus for privately owned, public open space. The generous amount of open space attracts people from the surrounding area, especially at lunchtime.

had the benefit of plenty of air and sunlight. This could best be achieved by setting buildings back from the street.

The Seagram Building, designed by Ludwig Mies van der Rohe and Philip Johnson for a block front on Park Avenue in New York City, illustrates this point of view. Indeed, its 200-foot-wide plaza that extends 80 feet from the sidewalk was a magnificent addition to the public realm, enjoyed as much by passing pedestrians as it is by office workers who sit along the plaza eating lunch, or by those who stroll across the plaza on their way into the building.

When the Seagram Building opened in 1958, it became the model for the "plaza" bonus that the New York City Planning Commission enacted three years later. Unlike Chicago, New York's bonus specified that to qualify for the bonus this open space had to be open to the public. The rationale for this requirement had to do with the building's impact on its immediate surroundings. Presumably, the additional open space was somehow related to the additional pedestrian traffic generated by the additional building floor area. Following the example of Chicago and New York, cities began enacting zoning laws that provided a bonus to property owners who set their buildings back from the property line, thereby creating more room for pedestrians.

Cluster zoning bonuses. A similar strategy was applied to the suburbs. Initially, land-use regulations had reflected Olmsted's design approach by requiring that houses be set back from the property line and from one another. It soon became clear that the resulting front, side, and rear yards were not really available for public use. Thus, in suburban areas the public realm increasingly became the highway and the street, often with no sidewalk.

When the Seagram Building opened in 1958, it became the model for the "plaza" bonus that the New York City Planning Commission enacted three years later.

Fairlawn, New Jersey, 1980.
In suburbs without adequate
public parks, streets and
driveways become actively
used locations for recreation.

Alexander Garvin

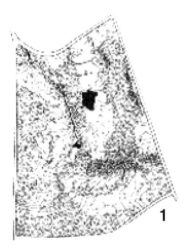

1

**Three alternatives for a Planned Unit
Development (PUD), New York City,
1968.** (1) Contour map showing existing
features (trees, ponds, creek, and
bounding road) of a 205-acre
undeveloped site. (2) Site plan showing
a conventional street grid (with 1,427
single-family house lots) that destroys
the natural character of the site. (3) Site
plan shows a cluster zoning scheme that
would preserve the natural features on
the site, provide for an elementary
school and shopping facilities, and
accommodate 1,445 housing units in a
range of building types.

2

3

Opponents of this form of suburban development and propo-
nents of preserving the country-
side denounced the resulting
cookie-cutter pattern of single-
family houses with identical
front, side, and rear yards. They
also objected to building place-
ment regulations that required
cutting down mature trees or
destroying interesting natural features. Obtaining government
approval for schemes that vio-
lated yard and setback regulations meant spending additional
time and money. Moreover, it
often reduced the number of
houses that fitted on a site,
thereby increasing costs.

One approach to solving this
situation allowed developers to
build more than the otherwise-
allowable number of houses, if
they arranged these houses in a
manner that retained attractive
landscape features and provided
common open space. This alter-
native to yard and setback
requirements, called planned unit
development (PUD) or cluster
zoning, began to be added to zoning ordinances and subdivision
regulations during the 1960s.

Presumably, the resulting common areas are better than cumulative total open space that would otherwise consist of small front, side, and rear yards. One has to wonder, however, about the rationale used by communities that provide a bonus (the right to build additional houses) to developers who provide such common open space. Is the right to build more dwellings than would be allowable under conventional zoning always justifiable by the ostensibly better site plan? What if the open space is hidden behind the houses or if the community is gated? Is the public realm truly increased?

Open space created in response to environmental concerns. Another approach relied on an age-old governmental responsibility: preventing actions that caused damage to other citizens. This approach took the form of legislation that required a review of the environmental impact of actions by property owners. If, upon review, a proposed project was shown to have a negative impact, mitigation could be required. That mitigation frequently was arrived at by negotiation among property owners, opponents to proposed development, and responsible public officials. In an attempt to comply with environmental policies, the developer of Northridge Hills in Danville, California, for example, erected walls to mitigate the traffic noise. The walls also increased the perception of security and the price the developer could charge. However, the landscaped parkway that was produced does not create a place where, as Olmsted would have recommended, "driving, riding, and walking can be conveniently pursued in association with pleasant people."

One has to wonder if the public realm is truly increased if the open space is hidden behind houses or the community is gated.

Alexander Garvin

Northridge Hills, Danville, California, 1995. Houses protected by masonry walls from "noisy" traffic on landscaped roadways do not create the parkway settings for genuine social interaction.

Florida, 1993. At the beginning of the twenty-first century, most American lived in suburban sections of complex metropolitan regions.

Irvine, California, 1998. Walled-in, gated subdivisions may provide safe open spaces. However, they need to be supplemented by parks, like this small park in Irvine, California, that provide recreational facilities for a variety of residents.

CITIES AND SUBURBS IN 2000

The nation's population is now 12 times as large as it was when Central Park was first proposed. Two-thirds of these 275 million Americans live in a metropolitan area, and most of them live in suburbs, rather than within the city itself (www.hud.gov). New York, with a population of 7.32 million in 1990, remains the largest city, but now it is one of 219 cities with populations larger that 100,000.

By any standard, the average American, who reported a household income of $34,076 in 1989, is prosperous (U.S. Census Bureau). Two-thirds of the households in the country live in a residence they own. Given the smaller household size of 2.6 persons and the growing size of dwellings, most people have more room to themselves. Thus, expanding the public realm does not seem as pressing.

The automobile has become a basic necessity for the 87 percent of households that own cars. But the simple city-suburb distinction is no longer a useful dichotomy for understanding how Americans live and work. Suburbs are now far more heterogeneous than they were in the first few decades after the Second World War. They no longer are restricted to the WASP country club set. Many Olmstedian suburbs with houses set back in the middle of ample yards have minority and working-class populations and some older, inner suburbs have deteriorated and need substantial reinvestment.

New suburbs continue to blossom on the edges of the spreading metropolis. Many are organized around common open space (sometimes encouraged by cluster zoning) and set apart by gates and security systems. In these new subdivisions, streets (especially when they do not include sidewalks) no longer function as places in which to interact with neighbors and meet people from other parts of town. Instead, people who wanted social interaction drive to shopping facilities that cater to people with similar interests. Kids hang out at the mall. The choice of places to go may have expanded. But many are privately rather than publicly owned and operated.

Alexander Garvin

Miami Beach, Florida, 1998. By the year 2000, millions of Americans spent time and money flying to places like Miami Beach for their vacations.

Competition with Parks

In such a prosperous society, with the average workweek having fallen to 35 hours, almost any recreational desire can be fulfilled. Americans spent more than $431 billion in 1996 on recreation. The vacation home business is thriving. Approximately 337,000 vacation residences were sold in 1999 (Reagor 2000). Travel by car, train, or even airplane is affordable and frequent—the average person thinks nothing of flying to a vacation across the country or overseas. In 1997, according to the Census Bureau, 52.7 million Americans traveled to foreign countries, a figure that was unimaginable in 1950, much less 1850.

All over the country, health clubs and privately operated gyms have been attracting a growing number of users. Commercial projects like New York City's Chelsea Piers Sports Complex provide insight into what we can expect. In 1992 the Chelsea Piers consisted of four forgotten piers extending 840 feet into the Hudson River. Today, it is a 30-acre sports and entertainment complex used by 10,000 visitors daily. The facilities that

In 1997, according to the Census Bureau, 52.7 million Americans traveled to foreign countries, a figure that was unimaginable in 1950, much less 1850.

Chelsea Piers Recreation Center

Chelsea Piers, New York City 1998. The recreation needs of millions of Americans are increasingly supplied by privately operated facilities like the Chelsea Piers Recreation Center, which offers golf driving ranges, rock-climbing walls, running tracks, ice rinks, swimming pools, and facilities for volleyball, boxing, bowling, basketball, and gymnastics.

To be sure, communities still acquire land for park development, especially underused waterfront land. But major park development initiatives, like those that were prevalent during the nineteenth century, are rare.

attract them include: 52 heated golf hitting stalls; the largest rock-climbing wall in the Northeast; a six-lane, 200 meter banked running track; two ice rinks, and major facilities for swimming, volleyball, boxing, bowling, basketball, and gymnastics. Although this sports complex operates on publicly owned piers, it is not a public park. The Hudson River Park Conservancy (see the section on Financing An Open Space Agenda in Part 2 below) leases the piers to the Sports Complex (a private, profit-making company that covers lease payments, maintenance, and operating costs out of annual memberships, user fees, rentals, sponsorships, and percentages from restaurant spending).

Television, the World Wide Web, shopping and entertainment centers, museums and galleries, professional sports: there are scores of alluring, private competitors for leisure time and money. Consequently, suburbs find it as difficult to raise the money needed to expand their inadequate parks systems as cities find it to pay for improving their poorly maintained facilities.

Not only do parks compete for leisure time; they compete for government spending with an ever-growing list of recipients. As the number of public programs has grown, so has the debate on the relative distribution of spending for debt service, public safety, education, welfare, and income redistribution programs. In such an environment, public spending on infrastructure and community facilities has increasingly receded. This is especially true of spending for parks. In 1963, for example, the New York City budget provided for 6,071 full-time Parks Department employees. By 1998, the New York City Department of Parks and Recreation documented that that number had declined to 1,156.

To be sure, communities still acquire land for park development, especially underused waterfront land. But major park development initiatives, like those that were prevalent during the nineteenth century, are rare. Few people (either in older cities with declining populations or in newer suburbs where houses are surrounded by front, side, and back yards) think parks should be a spending priority. The wonderful parks and parkways created during the nineteenth century are now old enough to be suffering from crumbling pavement, soil erosion, root exposure, worn-away plantings, and dead trees. As a result, the public dialogue in urban areas has shifted from expanding the public realm to maintaining it. Getting the money to pay for needed maintenance, repair, and replacement is even more difficult than generating public support for adding parkland.

New stadiums, arenas, and cultural and convention centers surely augment the public realm. But these facilities also draw away customers who might otherwise be spending time and money in public parks. Consequently, a large portion of funding that could have been spent on parks is spent on these other recreation facilities.

The gross amount of "open space" acreage in developing suburbs has been growing. However, much of this additional open space consists of wetlands, steep slopes, or other vulnerable natural sites. It is misleading to refer to it as *public* space. This is not land that is open to large numbers of people for active use. Thus, ironically, although the gross amount of open space has been growing, the amount of *parkland* available for public use has not been growing at a rate commensurate with the increase in population.

Community Decision Making

The political context in which the competition for leisure time and public spending takes place includes widespread community participation in decision making. Because a large number of voters doubt the effectiveness of government, their elected representatives are reluctant to increase taxes. Instead, they propose privatization as an efficient cure all or suggest that nonprofit organizations should play a greater role in many areas that used to be left to government.

The community revolution has devolved legitimate authority and power to a local level. This is not just the result of the urban renewal and highway battles of the 1950s or the poverty programs of the 1960s. At the dawn of the twenty-first century, Americans insist on a role in determining their environment. In many places, they believe that government has defaulted on its responsibilities. Since it did not or could not carry out those responsibilities, they are reticent about leaving the establishment, control, and maintenance of public space to government agencies. That is why neighborhood residents reclaim abandoned lots as community gardens and merchants reclaim neglected streets, sidewalks, and other public spaces by establishing business improvement districts.

Ronald Reagan's 1980 campaign mantra that "government is the problem" still resonates with many Americans. There has also been a concomitant but separate growth in the belief that individuals can better choose how to spend their money than government can. In such a political culture, there is little appetite for new public spending or higher taxes. As a result, private entities often finance, create, renovate, and maintain public facilities—everything from old parks to new museums.

Alexander Garvin

Alexander Garvin

It is becoming

increasingly clear that

government regulation

of private property is

a questionable way to

supply large numbers of

people with large

quantities of attractive,

usable open space.

PART 2

An Agenda for the Twenty-First Century

We have created a truly extraordinary network of public places: parks, parkways, playgrounds, and national forests. We also have put into place a complex regulatory system intended to make this public realm grow. It is time to discard those elements of the agenda that have become inappropriate, nurture and enhance those elements that will be increasingly valuable to future generations, make improvements, and pass on to the twenty-second century a public realm that is richer, more fulfilling, and more beautiful.

Government has a legitimate role as steward of the public realm. It is becoming increasingly clear, however, that government regulation of private property is a questionable way to supply large numbers of people with large quantities of attractive, usable open space. There are a small but growing number of land trusts that are adding property to the public realm. In some states, Colorado and California in particular, voters are beginning to approve ballot initiatives for increased public spending for property acquisition. Despite this good news, there remains no ground swell of national support for major spending to create substantial amounts of open space and even less support for diverting money away from schools and police to fund the operations of park agencies. Consequently, we will have to alter our approach both to regulation and to public spending.

It is futile to try to alter the myriad of property regulations that vary from political jurisdiction to political jurisdiction. But we do need to reach a common understanding of the situations in which it is appropriate for the government to require property owners to provide additional open space. We also need a better understanding of which regulations work and which don't.

31

Alexander Garvin

"Snake Hill Playground," San Francisco, 2000. Today, playgrounds, like this one in San Francisco, are so common that it is difficult to imagine a world without them.

Alexander Garvin

Hancock Center, Chicago, 1999. The plaza bonus at Chicago's Hancock Center has provided open space that is a genuine enhancement to public activity along North Michigan Avenue.

The success of the Olmsted agenda fooled us into thinking that all that was necessary to provide adequate parks was to acquire and develop open space, build community facilities, and operate recreation programs. This misguided thinking when combined with inevitably inadequate funding has produced a legacy of neglect. While we surely need to continue to increase the supply of public open space both in newly developing areas and in older cities and suburbs, we should be devoting the bulk of our energies to maintaining and improving what we already possess. The public realm itself needs to be better administered, repaired, rehabilitated, retrofitted, and repositioned. Fortunately, there are plenty of opportunities to reclaim abandoned property, redevelop obsolete areas, and integrate additional public spaces with a variety of other land uses. Elements of this new agenda have begun to appear around the country.

THE PRIVATE REALM— A REFORM AGENDA

The effort to extend the public realm onto private property has produced two unfortunate side effects. It has provided city governments and regional agencies with a rationale for avoiding further investment in the public open space. Why acquire and develop additional open space if property owners will provide public access to their land? It also has generated a property rights backlash that is beginning to imperil environmental laws and other protections.

Open Space Incentives

There is now sufficient evidence to demonstrate that we have not been able to satisfactorily enlarge the public realm on the cheap by offering bonuses for privately owned public space. Certainly some of the urban public spaces

Liberty Plaza, New York City 1997.
Liberty Plaza in lower Manhattan
provides "green relief" for thousands of
office workers.

*The effort to extend
the public realm onto
private property has
produced two
unfortunate side effects:
(1) a lack of investment
in public open space;
(2) a property rights
backlash.*

generated by plaza bonuses are
wonderful additions to the public
realm. Plenty of others leave much
to be desired.

Thanks to Jerold Kayden's
book, *Privately Owned Public Space:
The New York Experience* (2000), we
can evaluate four decades of experience in the city with the broadest
experience with open space incentives. New York City's Zoning
Resolution provides incentives for
arcades, covered pedestrian
spaces, open-air concourses, and a
variety of plazas and through-
block connections. As of the year
2000, there were 503 "privately
owned public spaces" in New
York City created in response to
zoning provisions. They cover
nearly 3.6 million square feet, an
area greater than 82 acres, mostly
on expensive land in Manhattan
(Kayden 2000). Some provide the
green relief Olmsted would have
admired. Others are wonderful
settings for social interaction.
Unfortunately, many plazas are
forlorn leftovers or hidden hang-
outs. The City Planning Commission has continually modified
applicable regulations in an effort
to improve the quality of these
public spaces. Their efforts have
met with limited success.

The record in suburban areas is
tougher to evaluate. There exists
no compendium of these open

Sony Plaza, New York City 1996. New
York City's zoning bonus encouraged the
creation of enclosed open space within the
SONY (formerly AT&T) Center that attracts
large numbers of people of every age,
income level, and ethnicity.

CBS Plaza, New York City, 1997. The sunken plaza that surrounds the CBS
Building in midtown Manhattan attracts none of the busy pedestrian traffic along
Avenue of the Americas. The only places to enter the building are on the side street.

The most difficult question is whether publicly owned and managed open space is public if people are excluded?

Peter Coutts Village, Palo Alto, California, 1995. Common open space at Peter Coutts Village provides children and adults with play areas conveniently near their residences.

spaces. Many of those that were created in response to cluster zoning ordinances are both usable and convenient. In other instances so-called "common open space" is the area remaining after fitting the maximum legal number of residences on a site. By virtue of their location behind private residences, this common open space is very convenient to the occupants of surrounding buildings. The problem is that, for that very reason, it is not truly open to the public. In New York City, property owners who obtained floor area bonuses in exchange for creating an "urban plaza" are required to post plaques at each point of pedestrian entry that include a public space symbol, a tree-like image, the international symbol of access for persons with disabilities, and two-inch-high lettering announcing that it is "Open to Public." The same approach should be taken to suburban common open space that is the product of a cluster zoning bonus.

Requiring public access to open space is tricky. In 1970, when the Nollan family applied for a permit to enlarge a bungalow on a site facing the Pacific Ocean, the California Coastal Commission granted them that right provided the public would be allowed to pass through the Nollan's property on the way to the Ocean. The Supreme Court ruled in the case of *Nollan v. California Coastal Commission* that there was no "essential nexus" between private action to enlarge a bungalow and public access to the waterfront (107 S.Ct. 3141 (1987)). Rather, it was an attempt by government to obtain a public easement without paying for it.

Suitable Public Spaces

The most difficult question is whether publicly owned and managed open space is *public* if people are excluded? During the past 50 years, governments have

North Pointe Village, Reston, Virginia, 1998. Common open space at North Point Village in Reston, Virginia, has produced a more pleasant parking lot. However, large numbers of people cannot use it for active reaction.

acquired enormous quantities of such open space. It usually comes in the form of "protected natural areas." In fact, such environmental preserves can be the very antithesis of public parks. The fact that both are publicly owned is no reason to conflate the two. One is expressly *no people*, while the other is a habitat for a wide range of flora and fauna *including people*.

In many newly developing areas, it takes years for the owners of large properties to get permission to build. The approval process is fraught with conflict, often generated by environmental protection issues. For example, development of a large new community on the site of the 22,899-acre Otay Ranch, 14 miles southeast of San Diego was stalled because of concern for the future of the gnatcatcher, whose habitat could have been threatened by the presence of large number of people. Eventually more than half the site was designated "open space." But it is surely not all "public" open space. It is difficult to create a habitat preserve that also can accommodate large numbers of very diverse people and even more difficult to create a public park that can sustain endangered flora and fauna.

Usually, the issues are less clearly defined. The resulting open space, however, may be no more suitable for public use. Area residents frequently decry proposed real estate development as "sprawl." They spend considerable time and money fighting development. Eventually, the property owners settle by preserving wetlands and steep slopes. Such areas are difficult or expensive to subdivide into single-family house lots, or to develop as retail shopping, manufacturing and warehousing, or to use as sites for office complexes. They are equally difficult and expensive to transform into actively used public parks. When the controversy is settled, the combatants declare victory because 20 percent to 30 percent of the land has been set aside as "open space." It may be a natural area, but it is not likely to attract much public use.

Common Open Space and Access to Private Property

There is every reason to maintain regulations that insure minimum standards. How else can the public ensure adequate ventilation within privately owned structures or adequate light on public thoroughfares? Surely, we do not wish to resume nineteenth century tenement construction. We should be far more judicious, however, in the manner in which we define and regulate common open space and in the way we obtain

Wetlands and steep slopes are equally difficult and expensive to transform into actively used public parks. While they may be natural areas, they are not likely to attract much public use.

New Albany, outside Columbus, Ohio, 1996. By integrating landscaped vehicular roadways and jogging trails with a fee-paying golf course, the designers of New Albany outside Columbus, Ohio, have created a truly comprehensive system of open spaces.

Freemont, California, 1993. The common open spaces that are part of these residential subdivisions east of San Francisco Bay, provide little more than private walkways and swimming pools.

Celebration, Florida, 1998. The neighborhood parks in Celebration are bounded by local streets and thus clearly available for use by anybody passing by.

public access to private property. Equally important, we need to recognize the limits of regulation.

The quality of plazas, for example, is related less to the contents and wording of zoning regulations than to the excellence of the designer selected by the building's owner or the quality of the building's management. The same is true of the attempt to improve the quality of suburban subdivisions. As Olmsted explained: "We cannot judiciously attempt to control the form of the houses which men shall build, we can only, at most, take care that if they build very ugly inappropriate houses, they shall not be allowed to force them disagreeably upon our attention" (Schuyler and Censer 1992, 286).

Much more can and should be done to insure that the public benefits from common open space. Golf courses do not have to be gated or even hidden behind expensive houses. They can be a public amenity if, for instance, they are visible. In the planned community of New Albany, outside Columbus, Ohio, the golf course is encircled by a public road and a simple fence made of white, wooden cross pieces that are easy to see through. The result is open space that can be enjoyed by golfers *and* by everybody else who drives, jogs, bicycles, or walks by.

The same issue of public visibility applies to the swimming pools, tennis courts, children's playgrounds, and other community facilities in residential subdivisions. These amenities are usually intelligently linked to surrounding buildings and used in common by their residents. Not one penny of private or public money need be spent to open them to a broader market. They can be added to our inventory of public open space simply by requiring site plans that pull them out from behind the houses. That is the approach taken at Celebration,

Alexander Garvin

Axial park boulevard, Celebration, Florida, 1998. At Celebration, carefully planted wetlands accommodate both runoff and recreation.

We need to increase substantially the amount and usability of open space.

Florida, the new town designed by Jacquelin Robertson and Robert A. M. Stern for the Walt Disney Co. There, open spaces that are used primarily by the occupants of surrounding houses are separated from those houses by a public street. In this manner the residents get the benefit of a location opposite open space without excluding anybody from that open space.

In Celebration, land that is constrained by environmental obstacles is treated the same way. Drainage creeks and wetlands are strung together into Lakeside Park. Rather than encircling these waterways with expensive houses, the lake is ringed by walking trails, tennis and basketball courts, picnic tables, and other recreation facilities. In this way, a nature preserve becomes more than a protected portion of the area's ecosystem. It also becomes public open space used for recreation purposes by both residents and visitors.

The attempt to extend the public realm onto private property certainly has provided greater access to open space. But the change is marginal. If we are to keep pace with the explosion in demand for recreation facilities, we need to increase substantially the amount and usability of public open space. This cannot be done on the cheap through regulation. It can only be done by buying large amounts of land and improving the character, management, and use of our enormous existing inventory of publicly owned, publicly managed open space.

THE PUBLIC REALM—AN ACTION PLAN

Too often, parks, squares, streets, in fact, the entire public realm is dealt with like the contents of an attic—items stored away until needed. When they are taken out again, they appear out of date. Substantial sums have to be spent on their repair and readjustment. No managers of privately owned real estate could afford to squander such valuable assets. They continuously seek ways to enhance and expand their holdings.

Clever developers are forever finding opportunities that their competitors rarely perceive. Rather than allow these opportunities to be exploited for private gain, responsible public agencies should be seeking and exploiting them to enhance the public realm.

Any attempt to expand or enhance the public realm will fail if it is not responsive to market demand. There are simply too many competitors vying for every minute of leisure time. There also are too many competitors for every public dollar. Consequently, public agencies must improve the way they use their facilities, spend their money, and deploy their personnel.

Successful shopping centers are not allowed to deteriorate; they are subject to continual renovation. Nor do successful shopping centers maintain obsolete merchandizing techniques; they are forever being repositioned. The custodians of the public realm should manage their assets in the very same way.

Clever developers are forever finding opportunities that their competitors rarely perceive. They acquire obsolete nonresidential buildings and retrofit them as loft apartments. They find abandoned sites and reclaim them for residential, commercial, or mixed use. They purchase properties that could be producing greater revenue and redevelop them. They find ways of adding apartments to buildings whose revenues would otherwise be entirely dependent on commercial activity.

Opportunities of these sorts abound. Rather than allow these opportunities to be exploited for private gain, responsible public agencies should be seeking and exploiting them to enhance the public realm. Existing parks can be adjusted to better satisfy the demands of park users. Park agencies can improve maintenance through the use of the latest management techniques and reposition existing facilities so they are of greater utility. Unused publicly owned territory can be reclaimed for public use. Open space can be combined with other public uses. Government agencies should make aggressive use of these opportunities both in the ways they use public property and in the ways in which they interact with private property.

Adjusting to Changing Market Conditions

The Minneapolis Park and Recreation Board is particularly active in adjusting its properties and activities to the changing demands of the population it serves. The Board operates programs that seek to understand what neighborhood residents would like. It also actively seeks out residents who are not using park facilities and finds ways to entice them to nearby facilities. Most important, it keeps introducing new activities and facilities that increase the attractiveness of the park system and the city itself.

During the early part of the year 2000, the Park Board initiated a "Listening and Visioning Project" in Peavey Park. Peavey Park is a 7.6-acre park that opened in 1927. The Parks Board believed that Peavey Park played an essential role in the lives of the people who lived and worked in the surrounding community. It believed that the park both shaped and reflected that community. Because of the diversity of the

PEAVEY PARK: A CITY PARKS FORUM STUDY

At the first City Parks Forum, held in New Orleans, in November 1999, Sharon Sayles Belton, Mayor of Minneapolis, presented her city's case "problem." It was Peavey Park. Assisted by the superintendent of the city's Parks and Recreation Board and a representative from Hope Community, Inc., she explained the city's commitment to community dialogue. Using a $35,000 grant from CPF given to Hope Communnity, Inc. as a result of its participation in the Forum, the three project partners have launched listening and visioning sessions that go beyond park design. Their goal is to involve community residents in drafting a plan employing innovative urban design concepts to lay out high-density/low-income affordable housing and safe passageways through the community, with the park as a centerpiece. This concept plan will also be used to seek other grant money. If you want to know more about CPF, please go to www.planning.org, e-mail CPF's director, Mary Eysenbach, at cpf@planning.org, or call 312-431-9100.

Alexander Garvin

community, the Board also believed that the listening and visioning project would result in proposals that also might be appropriate to other facilities in other areas. For those reasons, it obtained a $35,000 grant from the City Parks Forum, administered by the American Planning Association, to involve the community in a dialogue that would discover what park users wanted and thereby influence the future of Peavey Park.

The Board sent out 2,300 invitations to people who lived or worked in a 4-block area surrounding Peavey Park. It held 18 "listening" sessions in which 181 participants made often quite different proposals for the park's redesign. These sessions included all sorts of people who used the park: children, parents, the elderly, gang members, neighboring property owners, local institutions, and even merchants who operated nearby stores. Demands for added facilities included accessible bathrooms, telephones, and operable drinking fountains. Some residents wanted greater attention devoted to the northern end of the park, which they identified as an area of "social problems." Others called for longer hours of operation. The most unexpected suggestion was for a large outdoor signboard that listed park activities and the times they were scheduled. At the end of the process, the staff tallied the responses, identified common themes, summarized the results, and began implementing some of the recommendations.

Everybody involved thought that the listening and visioning process was an effective way of determining what the people who use a park actually wanted. In fact, they recommended that the Park Board allocate its own funds for similar efforts in other communities.

The Minneapolis Park and Recreation Board is not a passive agency. It actively generates market demand. A prime example is its use of recreation workers. The Board employs 71 full-time, 1,151 part-time, and 150 seasonal recreation workers. They are expected to participate in neighborhood meetings and advisory councils, promote year-round recreational programs, and actively work with volunteer personnel.

Peavy Park, Minneapolis, 2000.
Neighborhood children brought together by the Peavey Park Listening and Vision Project created this collage as part of their effort to explain how they though the park should be changed.

Alexander Garvin

North Commons Park, Minneapolis, 2000.
The Minneapolis Park and Recreation Board
is repositioning and renovating this
playground in an effort to create a more
user-friendly environment.

Like all park systems,

New York has

experienced drastic

reductions in personnel.

Today it has one-sixth

the number of funded

positions that it had

40 years ago.

Most cities assign recreation workers to playing fields, playgrounds, and indoor recreation facilities. Minneapolis recreation workers are nominally stationed in a specific park. Much of their time, however, is spent outside that park going into residential neighborhoods and commercial districts, getting involved with kids, and bringing them to park facilities for activities that interest them, but, for one reason or another, they are not using.

At North Commons Park, a 25.7-acre park about 2 miles northwest of downtown Minneapolis, the Park Board has brought in major sports teams to work alongside area residents. It has installed basketball facilities with the help of the Timberwolves, the area's NBA team. It has brought in the Vikings, its NFL football team, to help with the football field. This activist approach may help to pay for new and rehabilitated facilities. But it also increases community interest in those facilities.

Minneapolis has demonstrated that it is not enough to create handsome parks and wait for people to use them. Public agencies must also keep trying to ascertain resident desires, actively promote those facilities among area residents, and involve them in their management.

Improving Management of the Public Realm

The least glamorous of the elements of any open space agenda is management. In a period of scarce resources—and park agencies are always short of money—effective administration is essential. Many park agencies are well run. One in particular, the New York City Department of Parks and Recreation, is demonstrating how to improve management and maintenance despite cutbacks in funding. In New York City, parks accounted for approximately 1.5 percent of the annual operating budget during the 1940s and 1950s, when Robert Moses was Parks Commissioner. By the 1990s, it had dropped to less than one half of 1 percent. Despite decreasing resources, during the past decade conditions have visibly improved in the 18 miles of beaches, 46 swimming pools, 16 golf courses, 6 skating rinks, and 1,570 parks, playgrounds, and public spaces the agency manages. One of the reasons for these improving conditions is that Commissioner Henry Stern has adopted management techniques made possible by contemporary technology.

Like all park systems, New York has experienced drastic reductions in personnel. Today it has one-sixth the number of funded positions that it had 40 years ago. In part, the Workfare Program has offset this deficit by providing the department with 3,000 persons who were formerly on public assistance. In part, it has also been offset by improved deployment of personnel. To be sure, the Parks Department is doing all the traditional things private companies do to improve its personnel. It actively recruits at major universities. As a result, it is attracting recent graduates from Yale, Harvard, Cornell, and other colleges that do not routinely supply municipal agencies with entry-level personnel. It operates a career-training program for all recruits and has instituted a rigorous program of staff performance review. The explanation for management and maintenance improvements despite major reductions in budget and personnel, however, lies in the department's use of computerized reporting and citizen participation.

Lots of park agencies operate inspection programs. Starting in 1995, New York City revolutionized its Parks Inspection Program by introducing hand-held computers. Up to that time, written summary statistics had been issued only at the end of spring, summer, and fall inspection seasons. Now, rather than laboriously documenting information on paper and duplicating and circulating reports, inspectors are able to input ratings into hand-held computers while out in the field. Upon returning to the office they upload the information into the agency database. Computerization allowed the Inspection Unit to operate two-week inspection rounds and maintain up-to-date information. More important, detailed site-by-site information is now available instantly to all parts of the agency. In 1999 the department replaced Polaroid cameras with digital equipment, which allowed staff to upload photos in every office and print them along with database information about a particular location.

The Parks Inspection Program has developed a computerized database for 943 playgrounds, 443 small parks, 505 ratable zones in the city's 157 accessible large parks, and more than 1,200 planted (GreenStreet Program) areas. They are divided into three categories: structure, landscape, and cleanliness. Structure includes sidewalks, paved surfaces, play equipment, safety surfaces, benches, and fences. Landscape is categorized into trees, lawns, athletic fields, horticultural areas, trails, and water bodies. Cleanliness features are litter, glass, graffiti, and weeds. Each of these is rated acceptable or unacceptable, and the inspector specifically cites items that are hazardous or needing "immediate attention" (City of New York 2000b).

Every two weeks, 145 sites are selected at random by the Division of Operations and Management Planning and visited by the Parks Inspection Program's six inspectors. Their computerized reports are distributed at upper-level management meetings along with digital photos of hazardous or unacceptable conditions. They form the basis for targeting spending to problem areas that need immediate remedial maintenance or long-term capital investment. As a result of these techniques the overall condition of ratable sites has risen from 47 percent acceptability in 1993 to 86 percent in 1998. Cleanliness is now 96 percent acceptable. During fiscal year 2000-2001, the Department will spend $215,000 on the Parks Inspection Program. This is slightly more than one-tenth of one percent of the agency's annual expense budget.

Involving consumers in park management has proven to be one of the most effective approaches to improving maintenance. In 1995, Commissioner Stern recruited Timothy Tompkins, a 31-year-old public servant, to organize and direct Partnerships for Parks, the department's effort to increase citizen, community, and private-sector involvement with local parks. By combining small grants, technical assistance, and community organizing, Partnerships for Parks has built grassroots constituencies that act as supporters, advocates, and gadflies for the hundreds of lesser-known neighborhood parks. Tompkins demonstrated that these constituencies will create the political will for greater public funding and ensure that this money is spent wisely and with appropriate community involvement. During the past five years, the Partnerships has created a database of 50,000 city residents and 3,200 organizations willing to work on a wide range of park projects, from picking up litter to installing new playground equipment. From 1995 to 2000, Partnerships awarded more than 250 grants totaling $350,000 to neighborhood groups; hosted 120 workshops to more than 1,500 community leaders, and attended more than 6,000 community meetings. In 1999 alone, it coordinated more than a half-million hours of volunteer projects involving 25,000 people. The Ford Foundation and Harvard's Kennedy School of Government awarded the Innovations in American Government Award for the year 2000 to Partnerships for Parks because it has demonstrated that mobilizing citizen initiative can generate resources and creativity that would not otherwise be available to a municipal agency.

Starlight Park, the Bronx, New York, 2000.
The photographs taken with a digital camera by parks inspectors showed trash littering the steps at a small park in the Bronx. Upon reinspection, documented by another photograph, the litter was no longer a problem.

New York City Department of Parks

By combining small grants, technical assistance, and community organizing, Partnerships for Parks has built grassroots constituencies that act as supporters for lesser-known neighborhood parks.

Old Orchard Shopping Center, Skokie, Illinois, 1960 and 1999. The 1960 photo (top) shows some of Lawrence Halprin's planting design. The repositioning of Old Orchard extended from 1993 to 1995. When it was finished, Old Orchard had grown to 1.8 million square feet, including a food court (above), a multiplex movie theater, and a new 200,000-square-foot department store for Bloomingdale's. What had been Montgomery Ward was now a two-level Nordstrom store, and Lord & Taylor had been expanded from 60,000 to 115,000 square feet.

Reducing graffiti or replacing missing bench slats may seem unworthy of consideration. Enhancing agency personnel and involving area residents in community park activities may seem of minor importance. Asking park managers to maintain not only a lawn, but also a constituency, to cultivate not only plants, but also trust may be difficult. But these are the activities that have allowed Commissioner Stern to make New York City parks a model for the twenty-first century.

Renovating and Repositioning Existing Assets

Owner-operators of successful shopping centers, like Country Club Plaza in Kansas City, continuously reposition their properties. They do so in response to inevitable physical deterioration, changing market conditions, and developing customer preferences. It is the only way to compete with more modern centers and catch up with newer retailing techniques. Thus, visitors to Country Club Plaza in 1996 shopped at a Barnes & Noble bookstore that in 1980 was occupied by Macy's department store.

Just as store occupants change, so do the marketing techniques and, as a result, store appearance, signage, and landscaping (Schwanke 1994). The only place one can still see Lawrence Halprin's 1956 planting design for the Old Orchard Shopping Center (in Skokie, Illinois, outside Chicago) is in photographs.

Like shopping centers, the public realm needs to be periodically updated if it is to remain relevant to an ever-shifting user population with ever-changing preferences. And like shopping centers, streets, squares, and parks, it suffers the same inevitable physical deterioration and needs repair and renovation. The realization that the public realm requires periodic reinvestment became increasingly evident during the 1990s, as cities as different as Miami Beach and New York spent hundreds of thousands of dollars repositioning pedestrian malls, public squares, and playgrounds.

In 1960, Lincoln Road in Miami Beach became the second street in America to be pedestrianized (the first was Burdick Street in Kalamazoo, Michigan) (Garvin 1996, 143). Civic leaders thought that eliminating motor vehicles would accommodate the increasing number of tourists who were then the city's principal customers. Morris Lapidus, the architect they selected to redesign the street, convinced them that getting rid of automobiles was not enough. He felt that Lincoln Road had to be filled with different colors, lighting effects, and ornaments if it were to attract customers to wander among its stores. His design featured landscaped islands that subdivided and decorated eight blocks of this 100-foot-wide street. The islands were planted with exotic shade trees. The paving was painted with black-and-white striped designs. Shade from canopies and covered arcades protected window displays from the sun. At first, the design attracted tourists. But, as Miami Beach lost out to more fashionable destinations, Lincoln Road became a seedy memento of a bygone era (Brambilla and Longo 1977).

In the late 1980s, conditions began to change. Depressed prices attracted Cuban-American and gay entrepreneurs who bought and renovated run-down Art Deco buildings, at first near the beach and then closer to Lincoln Road. They attracted a new and different tourist clientele. In 1984, the South Florida Art Center opened on Lincoln Road. It provided affordable studio and gallery space to local artists who transformed the area into a fledgling arts district. Next came the Miami City Ballet, the New World Symphony at a renovated Lincoln Road Theater, and a 788-seat performance hall at the restored Colony Theater (Houstoun 1997, 164-77).

Lincoln Road's heterogeneous combination of resilient merchants, pioneering artists, designers, and entrepreneurs joined forces with idealistic civic leaders. In 1994 they persuaded the Miami Beach City Commission to establish both a capital improvement district and a management services district for Lincoln Road. As a result, $16 million was spent on physical improvements (infrastructure, roadwork, and mall amenities). Lapidus's striped paving was restored and augmented with new shade trees, shrubs, flowers, and simple lighting fixtures. The management services district assessed adjacent property owners to pay for security, sanitation, and landscape maintenance personnel. As a result, Lincoln Road competes successfully for customers with such Miami area attractions as the Coconut Grove shopping district and the Bayside Festival Marketplace. Rents have more than quadrupled. At night the area's restaurants and nightclubs attract visitors from all over the metropolitan area.

The story of New York City's Greeley and Herald Squares is even more dramatic. The 9,830 square feet that constitute Herald Square were acquired by the city in 1846 when Broadway (then called Bloomingdale Road) was extended across Sixth Avenue, north of 34th Street. Greeley Square, its 13,715 square-foot twin, south of 33rd Street, was acquired pursuant to the Small Parks Act of 1887. During most of the twentieth century, the benches that lined the squares were full of people who worked in the district or shopped at some of the world's largest department stores, including Macy's, Gimbel's, and Orbach's.

Lincoln Road, Miami Beach, Florida, 1993. By the early 1990s, the Lincoln Road pedestrian mall was in disrepair.

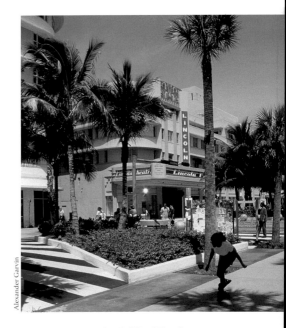

Lincoln Road, Miami Beach, Florida, 1998. A $16 million renovation repositioned Lincoln Road as a one of Miami's major restaurant and entertainment destinations.

BUSINESS IMPROVEMENT DISTRICTS

The earliest Business Improvement Districts (BIDs) appeared in the 1980s. They were created by downtown merchants and property owners who sought to compete with suburban shopping malls controlled by a single developer-owner-manager-marketer. The participants in a BID join forces to generate common action that they have no right to do individually or cannot afford to do. The activities of a BID go further than the common marketing activities by a merchants association (e.g., late night opening agreements, Christmas decorations, and newspaper advertising). Typically, BIDs pay for security guards, sidewalk sweepers, trash removal, information officers, and a full range of capital improvements. These activities are paid for through a surcharge on real estate taxes, collected by the city government and spent by a board of directors consisting of site occupants and property owners from within the district. Some notable BIDs include Denver's 16th Street Management District, Philadelphia's City Center District, and Baltimore's Downtown Management District. In 1984, the Bryant Park Restoration Corporation, for the first time, applied this financing technique to management of a park.

From the 1960s onward, the Department of Parks and Recreation budget was regularly reduced. The department responded by cutting back on repairs and maintenance. Conditions in the squares gradually worsened. Naturally, people avoided these increasingly forlorn public spaces. At the same time stores along 34th Street lost customers and property owners were unable to charge prime rents. In 1992 property owners and merchants joined to form a business improvement district (BID). The 34th Street Partnership more or less covers the area from 31st to 35th Streets, between Park and 10th Avenues.

The Partnership was determined to create a new image for the area. Herald and Greeley Squares became an important part of this effort. In 1996, it reached an agreement with the Department of Parks to assume responsibility for the squares. The Partnership spent $2.5 million on new lighting, benches, water fountains, public toilets, trees, shrubs, and flowers. Its annual budget for 2000 is $7 million, raised from an assessment of 25 cents per square foot of commercial floor area, 16 cents per square foot for retail, and 10 cents per square foot for residential. It is spent primarily for maintenance workers and security personnel. The BID spends more than twice what was being spent by the Department of Parks in 1996 when it took responsibility for the squares. As a result of these expenditures, hundreds of people are again spending time in Herald and Greeley Squares (Biederman 2001).

New York's Bryant Park is perhaps the most dramatic example of what can be achieved through renovation and repositioning. For decades, this six-acre park, right behind the New York Public Library on Fifth Avenue at 42nd Street, had been a treasured, quiet island of green surrounded by a wall of asphalt, concrete, steel, and glass. The original formal design had been updated in the 1930s, when material from the construction of the Sixth Avenue subway was used as fill to raise the level of the park. Elevating the park four feet above grade, enclosing it with shrubs which soon blocked views into the park, and providing only a few stairway entrances isolated Bryant Park from passing pedestrians and, more important, from passing police patrols.

The Parks Department, faced with continual budget cuts, deferred maintenance. Laurie Olin, the designer responsible for the park's later re-landscaping, described the situation very well: "Trees overgrown; ground beaten bare; trash overflowing the waste cans; stuffed into the long-abandoned light boxes; lights broken off and missing; pavement not repaired;

Herald Square, New York City, 1995 2000. (Below) Because of Parks Department budget cuts, Herald Square slid into disrepair. (Right) Substantial spending on capital improvements, maintenance, security, and sanitation made Herald Square an attractive sitting area for people who work and shop in the area.

Alexander Garvin

Bryant Park, New York City, 1996. On a typical summer Sunday afternoon, hundreds of people hang out at Bryant Park even though most area offices are closed and the nearest residential buildings are more than half a mile away.

Bryant Park, New York City, 2000. Making the entry areas to Bryant Park open and inviting encourages people to walk through and spend time there.

Bryant Park, New York City, 2000. The café at Bryant Park attracts visitors who would not otherwise be there.

hedges allowed to grow up to hide the ugly lights, themselves neglected and ugly" (Thompson 1997, 8). Eventually, Bryant Park became a dangerous place. In 1973 the Parks Department started closing park entrances with wooden police barricades every night at 9:00 PM. Three years later, the park's first murder occurred. The following year another murder spurred an effective reaction. Andrew Heiskell, chairman of the New York Public Library that bounded Bryant Park, asked William H. Whyte to analyze the situation (for a discussion of Whyte's principles, see Whyte 1980). Whyte's report stated:

- what everybody knew—the park was "dominated by dope dealers";

- what they unconsciously understood—"the basic problem [was] underuse"; and

- what very few people were ready to admit—the solution was redesign (Thompson 1997, 21).

The redesign Whyte proposed included removing iron fences and shrubbery, facilitating pedestrian circulation by providing additional entry points, and relandscaping. What finally emerged is largely the work of Hanna/Olin (overall landscape design), Hardy, Holtzman, Pfeiffer (new structures), and Lynden B. Miller (plantings). Central to its success was the construction of a cafe, restaurant, and kiosks. These new facilities attracted people who would otherwise have had no reason to be in the park. They would never have come, however, if Bryant Park had not become a beautiful, safe haven visible to pedestrians, taxi drivers, and to anybody passing by.

Bryant Park became a beautiful, safe haven. . . .

Sauer Playground, New York City, 1994. Once Sauer Playground had been repositioned and renovated by the New York City Department of Parks, it helped to trigger other neighborhood improvements.

Twelfth Street, New York City, 1988. Prior to renovation, Sauer Playground attracted activities that the Twelfth Street Block Association was determined to eliminate from the neighborhood.

Residents wanted to reposition Sauer Playground to "feel like a garden in the city."

It would be easy to dismiss these success stories as the product of money generated from prosperous retail districts. However, this repositioning strategy is as applicable to low-income neighborhoods. But, rather than property owners and merchants determining how to reposition the public realm, area residents determine what is to be done.

In 1993, the *New York Times* (12 September) described the block of 12th Street on Manhattan's Lower East Side containing the Joseph Sauer Playground as a place "where three-quarters of the children live below the poverty line, a street of worn tenement buildings and bodegas with red and yellow awnings, [where] caramels and condoms are sold behind bulletproof glass." The playground was one of nine sites acquired in 1933 with money from a World War I memorial fund established in 1921. It was one among the literally hundreds that Robert Moses developed with public works funds appropriated during the New Deal.

Like Greeley and Herald Squares, Sauer Playground was a casualty of the decrease in appropriations after Moses retired as commissioner of parks in 1960. The playground, as noted in the *Times,* "declined 'poca a poca' as neighbors say in the 1970's. No one remembers exactly which affront finally ignited the eight-year crusade. Was it the addicts shooting up and selling syringes? Was it the prostitutes—four in a three-block radius—turning tricks in broad daylight while children walked to school? Was it the out-of-state cars lined up to buy drugs on Friday nights? Or was it the Krazy Glue the pimps and crack dealers poured in the locks so that the people couldn't get into their own playground?" (Patricia Leigh Brown: "Reclaiming a Park for Play," *The New York Times*, September 12, 1993, The City Section, p. 1).

The crusade to salvage Sauer Playground began in 1986 when residents formed the 12th Street Block Association. It took them two years to get Commissioner Stern to include the playground in the agency's capital budget request. At first the City Council failed to appropriate the money. In 1989 residents persuaded the city to tear down two former crack houses that bordered the playground and to add the property to the site. Finally, in 1991, $530,000 was appropriated for renovation. Two years later the park reopened.

Residents opposed what they termed a "low-income neighborhood design." They wanted to reposition Sauer Playground to "feel like a garden in the city," with "lots of soft, safe, squishy surfaces" for younger children, "shade trees and comfortable benches for older people, and a sprinkler for cooling off in summer." Residents help with maintenance, locking the park at night, and reopening it in the morning. The playground remains in good condition because, like Lincoln Road, and Herald and Greeley Squares, its design and operation is responsive to user demand.

Reclaiming Territory for the Public Realm

Opportunities for enhancing the public realm open up when changes in population or economic conditions render previous land uses obsolete. For several decades, city governments have exploited these opportunities by reusing a wide range of abandoned and underused waterfront areas, streets, highways, and railroad properties. These projects offer exciting models for built-up areas where increasing the amount of public open space is erroneously thought to be difficult and expensive.

The waterfront is a case in point. During the eighteenth and nineteenth centuries, fleets of barges carried goods to warehouses and factories that lined the waterfront of major American cities. Between 1900 and 1910, more than 15 ferry lines moved people from both sides of New York's East River. The piers that remain have long since ceased to be used for maritime purposes and nearby upland sites are no longer as valuable. It has been decades since any American city waterfronts have been as extensively used. Not only is the water inaccessible in many places, it sometimes isn't even visible from nearby streets.

We may regret the loss of waterfront-related blue-collar industries. Their loss, however, provides a rare opportunity to re-open our shores and re-use the waterfront for people-oriented uses, rather than transportation, warehousing, and manufacturing. The Chicago Park District, for example, created 12-acre Ping Tom Memorial Park from surplus railroad property bordering the Chicago River. Detroit's Chene Park was created on property along the Detroit River that was once used by pharmaceutical, stove, and tobacco companies. Denver has been clearing away

Rotting piers, Staten Island, New York, 2000. Throughout the United States, there are thousands of piers, like these on Staten Island, that have ceased to be used for maritime purposes and could be reclaimed for recreational uses.

Ping Tom Memorial Park, Chicago, 2000. Chicago's Ping Tom Memorial Park is one of dozens of waterfront sites around the country that have been transformed into public parks.

Chene Park, Detroit, Michigan, 1998. The city of Detroit created Chene Park on a waterfront site abandoned by former manufacturing, storage, and shipping users.

Detroit River, Detroit, Michigan, 1990. Manufacturing uses along the Detroit River that were once dependent on shipping by water have moved to sites that provide more convenient access for trucks.

Cherry Creek, Denver, Colorado, 2000. The banks of Cherry Creek, once a manufacturing and warehousing haven, have been transformed into a linear park that is actively used for jogging, roller blading, and bicycle riding.

Confluence Park, Denver, Colorado, 2000. Confluence Park on Denver's Cherry Creek attracts large numbers of whitewater kayakers.

rubble and trash in order to create a series of parks along the Platte River. Similar redevelopment efforts are underway in Cleveland, Louisville, and other cities in which abandoned waterfront property is being used as dumps and junkyards.

Waterfront land is often seriously polluted. That was the situation in 1994 when the National Park Service began the restoration of Crissy Airfield, a 100-acre property along San Francisco Bay, east of the Golden Gate Bridge. The airfield was established in 1921 and played a vital role in the development of military aviation before it was abandoned and became part of the Golden Gate National Recreation Area.

The Crissy Field Restoration Project was completed in 2000. It required the removal of 86,000 tons of soil-contaminating, hazardous substances. The restoration, which cost approximately $32 million, transformed asphalt paving, roads, buildings, and eroded beachfront property into 28 acres of grassy field, 20 acres of tidal marsh, 22 acres of visitor amenities, and 30 acres of improved promenade and beach. The tidal marsh that had been filled after many years of military use is now once again being flushed naturally by the twice-daily rise and fall of tides in San Francisco Bay, by the influx of fresh water from the Presidio's Tennessee Hollow, and by clean stormwater from several outfalls (www.nps.gov/goga).

The design uses low-maintenance, drought-resistant plants and durable materials, reconfigures dunes, and reintroduces approximately 400,000 native plants. More important, it sustains itself in precisely the way that Olmsted recommended, by protecting ecosystems against the harm of human intrusion while opening up the natural environment for the enjoyment of large

Crissy Field, San Francisco, 2000. The reclamation of Crissy Airfield transformed roads and abandoned buildings into a sustainable tidal marsh and beach.

numbers of people. Crissy Field has become an ecological system that simultaneously provides a wide range of flora and fauna with a nourishing habitat and thousands of city residents with picnic grounds, benches and tables, restrooms, outdoor cold-water showers, overlooks, boardwalks, bike lanes, and parking.

Flood protection also offers an opportunity to make once-dangerous waterfronts publicly accessible. The Paseo del Rio, or Riverwalk, in San Antonio is a good example. In 1921 the San Antonio River flooded, causing 51 deaths. Engineers proposed relegating the horseshoe-shaped, downtown section of the San Antonio River to a concrete conduit and creating a new downtown street by paving over it. Instead, citizens demanded that the riverfront be transformed into a public park. Money for this project became available in 1939 when the Works Progress Administration (WPA) agreed to provide $300,000 if the city put up $75,000. The city raised the needed matching funds by issuing bonds.

When the park opened in 1941, it solved the flooding problems by dredging a bypass channel across the open end of the horseshoe and installing locks at either end. The locks are closed whenever necessary, so that floodwaters can be channeled away from the riverfront park. The riverfront, once dominated by factories and warehouses, now includes hotels, restaurants, and boutiques. It is the second most important tourist destination in San Antonio, after the Alamo.

Crissy Field, San Francisco, 2000. The parkland that replaced Crissy Airfield includes large areas used for active recreation.

San Antonio, Texas, 1997. San Antonio's Paseo del Rio (Riverwalk) has been transformed from a flood hazard into a major tourist destination.

Alexander Garvin

Wagner Triangle, New York City, 1998 and 2000. The GreenStreets Program has reclaimed this unused traffic island (left) and turned it into a small garden (above).

New York City Department of Parks and Recreation

Clairmont Street, New York City, 1998 and 2000. This bare space (bottom) has been reclaimed as a green island (top). Such islands provide valuable food, colorful berries, and links to larger habitat areas in public parks and other open spaces.

Alexander Garvin

New York City Department of Parks and Recreation

The Paseo del Rio is a model for the adaptive re-use of waterfronts as active public parks that attract large numbers of people. These potential customers attract developers, whose projects often bring new life to abandoned sections of our cities. The real estate tax payments that are generated are often sufficient to cover debt service on park development as well as operating costs of the park itself.

Opportunities for providing additional green relief are also available wherever vehicular traffic does not require all the space allocated to it (e.g. empty traffic circles, barely used sections of parking lots, and overly wide right-of-way). These unused, paved areas can be transformed into pleasant island gardens with trees, shrubs, and flowers, if they include curbs and sidewalks to protect planted areas from contaminated runoff. Such areas, however, must be free of such constraints as underground utilities, vaults, and light posts.

In 1996 the New York City Department of Parks and Recreation identified 2,700 such sites and established a Greenstreets Program to reopen them to public use. As of July 2000, it had reclaimed 1,100 of these sites, transforming them into island gardens that average 2,200 square feet in size. The department landscapes these islands with trees, shrubs, and groundcover that require a low level of maintenance and have a high tolerance of urban environmental stresses, such as drought, soil compaction, and pollution.

Just as city streets can be reclaimed, so can highways.

Paved surfaces create harsh heat islands that increase the release of gases and particulates into the air. Consequently, cities that replace these paved surfaces with extensive inventories of planted islands provide significant environmental benefits. The new cluster plantings create microclimates that reduce ambient air temperatures by as much as two to four degrees and provide cleaner air by filtering particulates and absorbing gaseous pollutants (Schwab 1992). Green islands also enhance cities as wildlife habitats by providing valuable food, colorful berries, and links to larger habitat areas in public parks and other open spaces.

Just as city streets can be reclaimed, so can highways. Perhaps the most dramatic example is Freeway Park in Seattle. The site was created in 1965 when Interstate 5 cut through the city dividing the central business district from nearby commercial and institutional land uses. These then-separated sections of the city were first reconnected in 1976 when a five-acre park was built over the highway. The design by Lawrence Halprin & Associates offers a wide variety of places where children can play, parents can sit and gossip, downtown workers can stroll, and everybody can escape the hustle and bustle of the city. In 1984, a two-acre section was added to it, followed in 1989 by the Washington State Convention and Trade Center. The combination has increased the attractiveness of sites for office buildings and retail stores in the business district to the west of the freeway and for residences and institutions to the east.

Freeway Park, Seattle, Washington, 1997. Freeway Park, built over an interstate highway, provides lovely settings for passive recreation while also reconnecting separate sections of downtown Seattle.

Kansas City, Missouri, 1994 and 1997. By removing old rails (right) and covering the site with crushed limestone, the abandoned trolley line that once served the Country Club District of Kansas City, was transformed into a public park (above).

Cedar Lakes Park Trail, Minneapolis, 2000. (Right) At Cedar Lakes Park Trail, planting a wide variety of native plants turned an abandoned rail yard into parkland. (Below) Three parallel, serpentine, asphalt trails for bicyclists, skaters, walkers, and joggers were combined with an operating railroad right of way to create Cedar Lakes Park Trail.

The decline in rail operations has opened wonderful opportunities for expanding the public realm by reusing for recreation purposes property freed by cuts in service. Sometimes the cost of reuse can be quite minimal. The trolley line that once served the Country Club District of Kansas City is a good example. All that was necessary to transform it into a public park was removing the old rails and covering the site with crushed limestone. More often, reclaiming unused railroad property requires vision and substantial sums of money. One of the most inspiring examples is Minneapolis' Cedar Lake Park and Trail. This three-mile long trail-*with*-rail connects restored and replanted meadows, marshes, forests, and waterways with a wide range of urban detritus including highways, relay towers, rail tracks, and parking lots.

The effort to create Cedar Lake Park and Trail began in 1986 when the Burlington Northern Railroad began dismantling a rail yard southwest of downtown Minneapolis. Developers quickly made plans to acquire and develop low-density subdivisions. Alarmed area residents formed Save Cedar Lake Park, later renamed the Cedar Lake Park Association, Inc., to persuade the Park and Recreation Board to acquire the property. By 1991, the group had raised $533,000 that, when combined with $1,067,000 appropriated by the State of Minnesota, allowed the Park Board to purchase 48 acres from the Burlington Northern (Harnik 1997a).

The design, by Jones & Jones/Richard Haag Associates of Seattle and Balmori Associates of New Haven, was intended to protect and improve water resources, reconstitute a wide variety of native plant life, connect ecosystems, integrate surrounding land uses, and celebrate people living in harmony with nature and one another. These objectives were achieved by eliminating the yard, retaining an operating railroad right-of-way, and adding three parallel, serpentine, asphalt trails that meander past low prairie ridges, wide swales, and shallow pools. Where the property narrows, the two one-way lanes for bicyclists and skaters merge with the third trail otherwise set aside for walkers and joggers.

Creating the newly landscaped Cedar Lake Park and Trail cost another $1,876,000. It opened in stages and was completed in 1997. By that time it was used on an average day by more than 700 bicyclists, three-quarters of them for commuting to work. They share the park with the usual array of people interested in more passive forms of recreation (e.g., bird watching and exploring wildflowers). The success of this project has spurred efforts to create a similar trail-*with*-rail along a corridor once used by the Milwaukee Railroad, and to continue adding greenways connecting even more of Minneapolis's extraordinary 6,400-acre park and parkway system.

The most surprising reclamation of abandoned property during the past quarter century has been as haphazard as it has been significant. Beginning in the 1960s, property owners abandoned unprofitable slum properties in cities as different as Boston, Detroit, and Chicago. Neither they nor their mortgagees believed these buildings were worth even unpaid real estate taxes. Local governments repossessed them for failure to pay taxes. In many cities the amount of abandoned property owned by local governments was staggering. By 1980 New York City had acquired an inventory of 46,420 apartments in occupied buildings (NYC Citizens Housing and Planning Council 1995). Every year it continued to acquire more abandoned property. Some buildings were sold, often to the tenants. But, like so many other cities, New York City was forced to tear down buildings that had become fire and safety hazards. In Philadelphia alone, 21,400 residential structures were demolished between 1970 and 1990. As a result, 9,500 of the 23,000 city-owned properties were vacant land (Harnik 1997b).

While some neighborhood residents worried about the impact of the activities that took place on these ill-maintained, city-owned lots, others saw them as opportunities. They took possession, sometimes illegally, sometimes pursuant to a month-to-month lease, sometimes as permanent managers. What emerged were "community gardens." Sometimes they featured handsome floral displays, sometimes expensive or difficult to obtain herbs and spices, sometimes vegetable patches that supplied a bounteous harvest of zucchini, tomatoes, and other fresh produce. But in all cases, they replaced neighborhood hazards with locally managed and maintained open space.

No doubt, community gardens have played an important part in reclaiming dilapidated neighborhoods. They do, however, require tough public policy decisions. Community gardens need to be supervised. Self-selected supervisors are often better motivated than government employees. Unlike city workers, volunteers are usually unpaid. In such circumstances, to whom are they accountable? Community gardens must be fenced and locked when not supervised. How then does a city prevent these gardens from becoming the private preserve of those who have keys? During how much of the day should they be open to the public? How can this be guaranteed? What happens when public officials consider replacing interim uses, such as community gardens, with permanent facilities, such as affordable housing? These are only some of the more important issues that cities will have to resolve if they are to have successful community garden program.

The most surprising reclamation of abandoned property during the past quarter century has been as haphazard as it has been significant. What emerged were "community gardens."

6th Street and Avenue B, New York City, 1986. In the 1980's many of the properties along Avenue B had been abandoned or had slid into a sorry state of disrepair.

6th Street and Avenue B, New York City, 1997. By 1997, the corner of 6th Street and Avenue B had been transformed from an abandoned lot into a permanent community garden, nearby buildings had been rehabilitated, and ground-floor retail space was filled with stores and restaurants.

6th Street and Avenue B, New York City, 1997. The Community Garden at 6th Street and Avenue B includes tomato plants, herbs, and a charming Children's Garden.

In most instances, community gardens have spurred second growth in low-income areas whose future was thought to be hopeless. Whenever areas of crime and blight are replaced by meticulously cared for gardens, surrounding properties are bound to be enhanced. This is what happened on the northwest corner of Sixth Street and Avenue B on New York's Lower East Side.

The city neglected its property at Sixth Street and Avenue B, as it did with properties at thousands of other locations. It became a convenient dump for private demolition debris and garbage. In 1983 a resident noticed a tomato plant growing in the rotting garbage and persuaded the Sixth Street Block Association to take charge of the site. Within a year, it had negotiated a lease with the city, cleared the garbage, and started a garden. Area residents fenced the lot, installed benches and picnic tables, a small playground, vegetable and flower gardens, and a compost heap. With help from the Trust for Public Land and the City of New York's Green Thumb Program, area residents established Sixth Street and Avenue B Garden Inc. In 1996 it took permanent possession of what had become a significant neighborhood asset.

The Sixth Street and Avenue B Garden is not the only community garden on the Lower East Side. Several dozen others sprouted at other city-owned sites. They began to change the perception of the neighborhood. As the crime rate began to fall throughout New York City, newcomers began to be attracted by low-rent, "fixer-upper" tenement apartments. With assistance and substantial subsidies from the city's Department of Housing Preservation and Development, nonprofit and even some profit-motivated developers started building "affordable" co-op row houses and apartment buildings. Enterprising business people began replacing store-fronts that once housed drug dens with bistros, bars, and cafés. Conditions have changed so completely that on December 24, 2000, the *New York Times* reported that "marketers of high-priced condominiums and luxury rentals that are sprouting everywhere in the neighborhood are more likely to refer to it as the East Village."

Combining Public Open Space with Other Functions

Too many cities think of parks in a single-function manner. Instead, where appropriate, they should be combining recreation with other public facili-ties. Schools are an obvious example. Some of the more unusual combina-tions occur when recreation is combined with drainage and when parks are combined with motor vehicle storage or other difficult to locate facilities.

Storm runoff can be a serious problem if it is not dealt with intelligently. In 1914 the Los Angeles River overflowed, causing $10 million in damage. Engineers recommended channelization into a concrete culvert. The Olmsted Brothers and Bartholomew and Associates in their 1930 plan, *Parks, Playgrounds and Beaches for the Los Angeles Region*, argued instead for combining flood control, water conservation, and park development. The proposal, they explained, would "at little extra cost" create "parks along natural drainage lines on lands relatively cheap, and extensive enough for recreation purposes." Essentially, the idea was to create parks that, during sudden periods of flooding, could hold the water, allowing it later to flow away naturally. This combination, they believed, would "lead to an ampler and better solution of both problems at much lower cost of con-struction than either would separately pay" (Olmsted Brothers and Bartholomew and Associates 1930).

The Olmsted Jr./Bartholomew park-drainage proposal was part of an ambitious regional plan that at the time was estimated to cost $230.1 mil-lion, seven times the budget of the entire city of Los Angeles (Gumprecht 1999, 268). The plan was released five months after the stock market crash that triggered the Great Depression, not an auspicious time to finance a proposal of this magnitude. No action was taken.

Storm runoff problems continued to plague the area. In 1934, floods caused 40 deaths; in 1938 floods caused 59 deaths. The city's solution was to relegate 46 miles of the Los Angeles River's 58-mile route through the city to concrete culverts fenced off from the public. Today, Los Angeles no longer experiences serious flooding. By investing in a single-function capital improvement, however, the city missed its opportunity to create a rich and varied 58-mile public park that also solves an environmental problem.

Too many cities think of parks in a single-function manner. Instead, where appropriate, they should be combining recreation with other public facilities.

Los Angeles River, Los Angeles, 1996. Much of the Los Angeles River flows through fenced-in concrete culverts identified by "no trespassing" signs.

Alexander Garvin

Boulder, Colorado, 2000. The Boulder Creek floodplain includes tree-lined pathways used for skating, jogging, and bicycle riding.

Boulder, Colorado, 2000. Fishing is a favorite activity at one of the minor waterfalls along Boulder Creek.

In the mid-1980s, a citizens group called Friends of the Los Angeles River was formed to convince public officials of the merits of the Olmsted Jr./Bartholomew approach. Their work is only now beginning to bear fruit. The Army Corps of Engineers has undertaken a project that will replace some areas of concrete with detention basins, use permeable materials like brick and cobblestone for driveways and parking lots, and install cisterns and dry wells to take in runoff. This will allow water to soak into the ground and make possible the creation of a more naturalistic landscape. The City of Los Angeles has begun reclaiming stretches for a Los Angeles River Bike Path. In 1999, the California Department of Transportation (CALTRANS) awarded $250,000 to the City of Maywood and The Trust for Public Land to help acquire a two-acre parcel of industrial property to add to the new Maywood River Park, which will provide five acres of public riverside recreation. In time the Los Angeles River may become the park envisioned in the early twentieth century. But it will surely be much skimpier, more difficult to create, and be far, far more expensive. It would have been much more cost-effective to proceed before development occurs and land costs skyrocket.

If the recommendations Frederick Law Olmsted Jr. made for Los Angeles may have seemed costly at the time and have yet to be realized, his similar, but far less ambitious, proposals for Boulder Creek were eventually implemented. In *The Improvement of Boulder, Colorado,* a plan he and Charles Eliot wrote in 1910, they argued that it would be "foolishness" to create a conventional, "highly polished and exquisite" park "with costly flowers and other decorations." A landscape of this sort "would be ruined by

Alexander Garvin

Alexander Garvin

Union Square, San Francisco, 1999.
The 2.6-acre park on top of the garage at San Francisco's Union Square provides green relief from surrounding commercial activities.

Combining car storage with parkland is another cost-effective way of obtaining public open space in high-density, downtown districts where land is expensive.

flooding" (Olmsted and Eliot 1910). Instead, they recommended retaining the bottomland created by centuries of Boulder Creek flooding. The proposed drainage system and park would consist of plain open fields with a few bushes and some "tough old trees" that provided areas in which children could play, residents could fish, and families could picnic. Others could stroll along a creek embankment on shaded paths that occasionally offered wonderful views of the foothills of the Rocky Mountains.

Although Olmsted Jr. and Eliot had proposed an extremely inexpensive means of dealing with drainage and flooding, it was ignored until 1983, when Spenser W. Havlick was elected to the City Council. Havlick was an admirer of the Olmsted Jr./Eliot plan. He asked the Boulder Department of City Planning to prepare a proposal for Boulder Creek, inspired by that 73-year-old document. The City Council funded their recommendations. Today, Boulder residents enjoy the combined drainage-recreation facility on which Los Angeles is only beginning to work.

Combining car storage with parkland is another cost-effective way of obtaining public open space in high-density, downtown districts where land is expensive. This is no new strategy. San Francisco pioneered it in 1940 when it created a 1,700-car garage under Union Square. Mellon Square in Pittsburgh covers an 896-car garage, Pershing Square in Los Angeles covers a 2,150-car garage, Memorial Plaza in Cleveland covers a 900-car garage, and Market Square in Alexandria covers a 236-car garage.

Post Office Square, Boston, 1999. People can walk through the 1.7-acre park without being aware that 1,400 cars are parked underneath.

One of the most successful recent examples is Post Office Square in Boston. When the city decided to replace a 950-car garage built in 1954, with a larger 1,400-car facility, it decided to store the cars on seven underground levels and create a 1.7-acre park on top. Post Office Square is different from most similiar facilities because it successfully integrates downtown pedestrian traffic into the park. Ellenzweig Associates, its designers, recognized that small center city parks had to be a part of the complex mix of activities that take place in downtown locations. They did not want it to be merely a refuge from the activities of its busy streets. Consequently, their scheme includes paths that offer pedestrian short cuts to the large buildings on one or another side of the square. There are plenty of sitting areas where office workers can eat a sandwich lunch or read the paper, and a café-restaurant where they can stop by to pick up coffee and a bagel on the way to work in the morning.

Post Office Square is different from most similiar facilities because it successfully integrates downtown pedestrian traffic into the park.

Post Office Square, Boston, 1999. Post Office Square provides sitting areas where office workers can eat lunch or read the paper and a café-restaurant where they can stop by to pick up coffee and a bagel on the way to work.

Los Angeles's Pershing Square demonstrates that simply building a park on top of a garage will not provide enough customers to justify the retail activity that is needed to animate such public spaces. Steps and walls obstruct easy entry into what is a far larger park. Unlike the café at Post Office Square, the café at Pershing Square does not open directly onto the sidewalk, nor is it easily visible from the sidewalk. Consequently, it is not able to attract enough pedestrian traffic. At Post Office Square, on the other hand, hundreds of passersby can see customer activity in the glass-enclosed café even after sundown. Consequently, Boston's garage-park is far livelier than Los Angeles's.

Riverbank State Park in New York City is perhaps the most startling combination of seemingly incompatible functions: a $1 billion sewage treatment plant covered by a 28-acre recreation center. The project became necessary in 1965 when the federal government ordered the city to cease dumping raw sewage into the Hudson River. It took the city three years to settle on a half-mile-long site on the river on the far side of railroad tracks and the six-lane Henry Hudson Parkway. Despite the facility's distance from upland residential areas, community leaders were outraged. They didn't want sewage treated in their neighborhood. After years of controversy, in 1980 they settled on covering the roof of the treatment plant with a state-financed public park to be designed by architect Richard Dattner.

Pershing Square, Los Angeles, 1996. The five-acre park that covers a 2,150-car garage is the fifth design for a public park that was established in 1866.

Pershing Square, Los Angeles, 1996. Major obstructions introduced by the 1994 design for Pershing Square block pedestrian views into the park.

Riverbank State Park, New York City, 1999. The 28-acre park, which covers the top of a pollution treatment plant that processes sewage from the West Side of Manhattan, provides major recreation facilities for residents of northern Manhattan.

Old State House, Baton Rouge, Louisiana, 1998. Like many public structures, the Old State Capitol in Baton Rouge is surrounded by attractive landscaped grounds that have had negligible impact on the surrounding city.

Cleveland, Ohio, 1999. There are few weekend users for the monumental open space around which Cleveland's major government buildings are grouped.

Lake Meadows, Chicago, 1993. The open spaces between buildings in mid-twentieth century urban renewal projects, like Chicago's Lake Meadows, may be generous, but they are little more than space that is left over after accommodating high-rise buildings.

By the time the facility opened in 1993, New York State had spent $129 million on Riverbank Park. Its facilities included softball, basketball, handball, tennis, paddleball, and football/soccer facilities, as well as running tracks, swimming pools, a skating rink, playgrounds, picnic areas, walkways, open lawns and shade trees, a cultural center, a café and restaurant, and a carousel. In its second year of operation, more than 3.7 million visitors annually were using Riverbank State Park.

Making Effective Use of Open Space in Public Projects

The public realm grows whenever government takes private property for a public project. During the nineteenth century, this open space was little more than a setting for public buildings. The Old State House in Baton Rouge, dedicated in 1849, is typical. Setting it back from the street enhanced the building. The surrounding greenery, however, added little to the daily life of the city.

Early twentieth century projects were more ambitious. Inspired by the Chicago Fair of 1893, project designers arranged public buildings so as to create monumental public squares. In doing so, they added acreage to the public realm. But it was not easily available for play. For example, the grand mall, around which are grouped Cleveland's City Hall, Courthouse, Post Office, Libraries, and Public Auditorium, is a vast decorative open space 560 feet across that attracts few people on weekdays and virtually nobody on weekends.

The green spaces included in mid-twentieth century urban renewal projects tended to be even more generous. They routinely included playing areas for small children and benches for the elderly. The space itself, how-

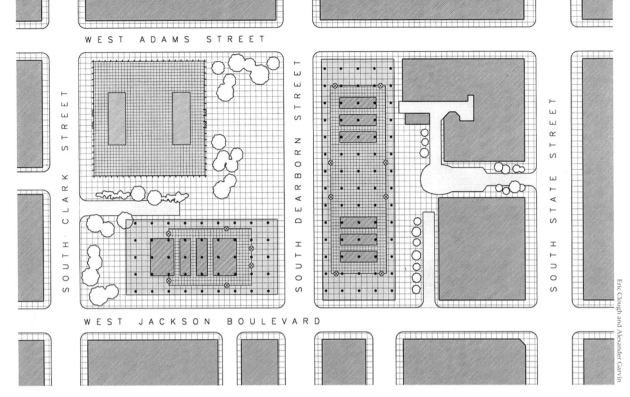

WEST ADAMS STREET

SOUTH CLARK STREET

SOUTH DEARBORN STREET

SOUTH STATE STREET

WEST JACKSON BOULEVARD

CHICAGO FEDERAL CENTER

Federal Center Plan, Chicago, 1959-1974. The two office buildings, post office, and public open spaces in Chicago's Federal Center are routinely used by thousands of people.

ever, often is little more than what is not used by the buildings. A small portion of the 70-acre site of Chicago's Lake Meadows redevelopment project, for example, is used for 10 apartment buildings containing a total of 2,033 apartments . The rest of the site is leftover green space.

These three very different open spaces are missed opportunities. Open space should not be thought of as an adjunct to the architecture. More recent government-sponsored projects have demonstrated that by placing buildings at strategic locations, public open space can be used to direct the daily flow of people in a way that integrates that open space into the daily life of the surrounding city.

Chicago's 4.6-acre Federal Center was begun in 1959 and built in three stages ending in 1974. It fills one entire block and a portion of a second, on either side of Dearborn Street. Mies van der Rohe, the designer of this redevelopment project, arranged its buildings in a manner that enhances downtown life. More than 14,000 people work in its two high-rise office slabs, one of which includes 12 floors of federal courtrooms. Together with thousands more who do business in court and in federal offices, or who visit the one-story-high Post Office with which they share the site, they generate substantial pedestrian activity (Carter 1999, 69, 132-35).

The Federal Center was designed to create a pedestrian-friendly environment for both building users and passersby. Adams Street and Jackson Boulevard, which bound the project on the north and south, are only 66 feet wide. In order to provide more light and air to the sidewalk along these streets, the office buildings are set back slightly from the property line. Conversely, both buildings extend to the property line along Dearborn Street, whose right-of-way is 80 feet across, wide enough to provide plenty of natural light. To entice pedestrians along all three streets, the sidewalk is extended under 26-foot-high building arcades.

Federal Center, Chicago, 2000. Mies van der Rohe arranged the buildings of the Federal Center in a manner that enhances downtown life.

Federal Center, Chicago, 2000. To entice pedestrians along all three streets, sidewalks are extended under the 26-foot-high office building arcades.

Alexander Garvin

Pioneer Courthouse Square, Nordstrom kids, Portland, Oregon, 1998.
The square is a magnet whose attraction has changed the city around it.

Pioneer Courthouse Square is a magnet whose attraction has changed the city around it.

The Post Office is set back 122 feet from Dearborn Street to form a public plaza animated both by Alexander Calder's large, freestanding, red-painted steel sculpture entitled *Flamingo* and by the activity that can be seen behind the glass facade of the Post Office. This space is linked by a broad walkway to a second public plaza at the corner of Jackson Boulevard and Clark Street. Both plazas are part of much larger volumes of space defined, not by property lines, but by the walls of the buildings across the street. Thus, not only is the Federal Center's pedestrian activity integrated with the rest of the city, so are its public spaces.

The Federal Center demonstrates how to make the open spaces between the buildings truly marvelous additions to the public realm. How much better when, like Pioneer Courthouse Square in Portland, Oregon, the open space itself becomes the magnet attracting people to the city.

Portland's 200-foot-by-200-foot blocks provide unusually convenient circulation. Nevertheless, civic leaders are forever finding ways to enrich the public realm. In 1977, Fifth and Sixth Avenues were transformed into redbrick transit malls with flower-filled containers, bubbling fountains, and public art. Nearly all of the city's 71 bus lines run along one of these two parallel transit malls. Eleven years later, Portland inaugurated a light rail line (MAX) along two parallel streets that crossed the transit malls and continued 15 miles into the suburbs. The block enclosed by MAX and the transit malls was sure to become one of the most valuable locations in Portland. It was unavailable for use as a public park because Pioneer Courthouse, a landmark structure, begun in 1869, occupied the site. Consequently, in 1979 the city purchased the next block west. It was occupied by a two-story parking garage that had replaced McKim Mead & White's Portland Hotel 28 years earlier.

Once the site had been acquired, the city held a design competition for a new public square to replace the garage. There were 162 submissions. A team led by Martin/Soderstrom/Matteson (architects) and Douglas Macy (landscape designer) submitted the winning project. Altogether, Pioneer Courthouse Square cost $7.3 million ($3 million for acquisition and $4.3 million for development).

Pioneer Courthouse Square opened in 1984. It attracted people from all over the metropolitan area. Some came for coffee at a café on the square, some to get transit passes from the kiosks under the square, some to purchase maps, books, or foreign exchange from Powell's Travel Store. Many people came to sit on the benches or just to hang out.

Nordstrom's built a new store opposite the square. The Rouse Company converted the nearby Olds and King Department Store into "The Galleria," a 75-foot high shopping atrium. Saks Fifth Avenue and Pioneer Place (a multistory shopping arcade) opened a block away. Additional buildings continue to be erected on the blocks around the square. Clearly, Pioneer Courthouse Square is not merely open space. It is a magnet whose attraction has changed the city around it.

Portland's 200-foot-by-200-foot blocks provide unusually convenient circulation. Nevertheless, civic leaders are forever finding ways to enrich the public realm.

Alexander Garvin

Pioneer Courthouse Square, Portland, Oregon, 1998.
Portland, Oregon, replaced a garage with a public park that fills an entire 200-foot by 200-foot block.

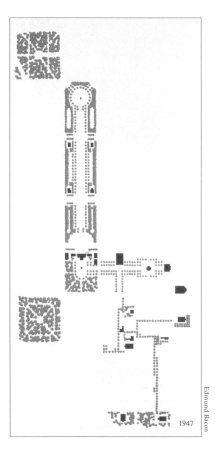

Greenway plan, Philadelphia, Pennsylvania, 1947. Edmund Bacon's original idea for Society Hill's greenways connected the area's historic structures.

St. Peters Walk, Philadelphia, Pennsylvania, 1998. The steeple of St. Peter's Church attracts pedestrians to use the greenway.

Society Hill, Philadelphia, Pennsylvania, 1999. Three Bears Park is one of the destinations connected by Society Hill's greenway system.

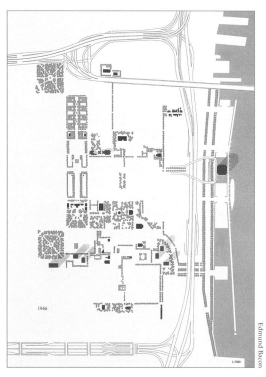

Greenway plan, Philadelphia, Pennsylvania, 1967. As built, the greenway system followed routes made possible by the acquisition of empty lots and sites with structures that were beyond cost-effective rehabilitation, or whose uses were incompatible with the surrounding neighborhood, or were necessary to complete a pedestrian access to significant destinations.

Philadelphia's Society Hill redevelopment project is well known as having transformed dilapidated buildings into a desirable upper-middle- income neighborhood. Too little attention has been directed to the small parks and pedestrian greenways that have helped to make Society Hill such a special place. The initial idea for this network of public spaces came from Edmund Bacon, who presented his initial greenway plan in 1947 at the Better Philadelphia Exhibition. Bacon, the city's planning director from 1949 to 1970, believed that this open space network, when combined with rehabilitation of more than 700 historic buildings and new construction strategically located throughout the areas, would sufficiently enhance the neighborhood to entice people to move there.

Decades later, when the redevelopment of Society Hill was completed, its open space network was remarkably similar to the one Bacon initially sketched out in 1947. It was assembled from:

- sites that had been empty lots;
- buildings in such poor condition that rehabilitation was not appropriate;
- properties occupied by land uses that were not compatible with a residential neighborhood; or
- sites needed to reach a particular destination.

Few districts had such a remarkable choice of destinations: national landmarks, local churches, and neighborhood playgrounds on every block.

Bacon's design had its roots in his memories of a teahouse that stood in the middle of a pond in Shanghai. To get to the teahouse you had to cross a series of bridges altering your direction in a zigzag pattern. Each time there was a change in direction, the experience of Shanghai changed. For this idea to be applicable to

Society Hill, Bacon believed there had to be a reason to change direction. Nobody would zigzag just for the fun of it. His solution was to terminate each greenway with a significant destination and then force a pedestrian to change direction in order to take the next greenway (Bacon 1998).

The open space network Bacon conceived, like the open space in Chicago's Federal Center and Portland's Pioneer Courthouse Square, includes magnets that attract users and employs surrounding buildings to enclose the public spaces. Like the Federal Center, it also integrates new and old sections of the city. More important, these spaces are knitted together in a manner that encourages people to wander through the neighborhood. The time they spend wandering becomes even more important than the open space itself.

Financing an Open Space Agenda

Park development is usually paid for out of government budgets. Public officials usually point out that these expenditures are justified because parks will increase real estate tax collections from neighboring properties whose value they enhance. Now that open space has to compete with so many other government objectives, open space advocates need more than a convincing rationale—they need dependable sources of financing.

The financing mechanisms that have proven to be particularly effective include dedicated lease payments, fees, real estate taxes, and sales taxes. In most cases, local governments insist on taking all tax revenue and making annual appropriations for park and recreation purposes. Minneapolis, Boulder, and Chicago are exceptions. Since 1883, Minneapolis has financed its park system primarily from a dedicated real estate tax. Boulder depends on a dedicated sales tax. Chicago has a separate taxing district for parks.

New York City in particular is using some inventive approaches for financing public open space. The city's new Hudson River Park depends on dedicated lease payments. It runs at-grade between the Hudson River and Route 9W from Lower Manhattan to 59th Street. When the Park is completed, it will include a 4.5-mile waterfront esplanade connecting 13 renovated public recreation piers, ball fields, playgrounds, boating facilities, and the Chelsea Piers Sports Complex. While the nearly $330 million capital cost of developing this new linear park will come primarily from city, state, and federal funds, its operating expenses will come from lease and concession revenues generated by properties along the right-of-way of Route 9W. The 34 piers that are currently leased to private companies annually generate $10 million in revenues, all of which goes to the park.

In 1984, the city created a Business Improvement District (BID) surrounding Bryant Park. At that time an additional annual tax payment equal to about 11 cents per square foot of floor area was added to the real estate tax paid by owners of the 7.5 million square feet of property surrounding Bryant Park (the payment amounted to 14 cents per square foot in 1999). It paid for all the physical improvements that resulted in its successful reclamation.

When the Department of Parks turned over maintenance and management of Bryant Park to the BID, it was spending $250,000 a year on the park. Spending in 1999 was $2.5 million. Of that, $950,000 came from the BID. Concession revenue, sales, grants, and parks rentals covered the rest. The money paid for two shifts of security officers, two shifts of sanitation workers, regular planting, and all aspects of management and maintenance (Biederman 1999).

The Department of Parks has created a series of nonprofit foundations to assist with park restoration and maintenance. The Central Park Conservancy raises $21 million annually. Few parks have the same number

When the Hudson River Park is completed, it will include a 4.5-mile waterfront esplanade connecting 13 renovated public recreation piers, ball fields, playgrounds, boating facilities, and the Chelsea Piers Sports Complex.

Hudson River Park, New York City, 2000. New York is creating a five-mile-long park along the Hudson River whose operating costs will be covered by lease revenue from publicly-owned piers and commercial properties that are part of the site.

Parks don't just appear; neither do they run themselves. Moreover, if leadership is mediocre, the results will be similarly mediocre.

of rich occupants occupying surrounding property and, thus, are unable to raise the large sums the public parks require. No parks system can rely on a steady stream of donations. However, these citizen-led institutions can raise money for projects that would be unlikely to come from the city budget. The Prospect Park Alliance, for example, raises more than $3 million a year for projects that otherwise would be unlikely to get city money. Among its more prominent efforts have been restoring the park's carousel and raising half the $10 million needed to recreate the Prospect Park Woodlands, which Olmsted and Vaux had designed to include cascades, ravines, and heavily wooded areas in which to completely escape from city life.

Implementing the Agenda

Parks don't just appear; neither do they run themselves. Moreover, if leadership is mediocre, the results will be similarly mediocre. The inspired entrepreneurship that parks require is not easy to come by. Central Park was lucky. Its admirable current condition is the result of the entrepreneurship of Robert Moses and Elizabeth Barlow Rodgers. As Parks Commissioner between 1934 and 1960, Moses inspired municipal officials and scrounged the money to restore, rebuild, and maintain the park. His successors were not as effective. During the 20 years after he left office, all New York City parks deteriorated badly. When Betsy Rodgers became Central Park Administrator in 1979, she saw opportunities that others had neglected. She brought in specialists to prepare plans for the park's restoration, used these plans to raise money to pay for the restoration, and in 1983 created the non-profit Central Park Conservancy to oversee both.

After Moses, Brooklyn's Prospect Park went through the very same decline that had occurred at Central Park. Its budget and staff also had declined to a level that was far too small to maintain the park. Raising money from individual and corporate donors was more difficult than obtaining contributions for Central Park. Prospect Park just doesn't have the same national corporations and wealthy residents occupying buildings in walking distance of the park. Nevertheless, Tupper Thomas, the Park's Administrator, made remarkable progress obtaining contributions for restoration and maintenance. She commissioned the first landscape studies and area restoration plans since the park's inception. They provided a blueprint for action, for fundraising, and for major work in sections of the park that had be neglected for decades.

The developers of the Chelsea Piers Sports Complex, Tom Bernstein, Roland Betts, and David Tewksbury, were convinced that thousands of people seeking recreation could be attracted to a waterfront location that had been long abandoned. Like any entrepreneurs, they perceived an opportunity that nobody else understood. They also perceived that annual memberships, user fees, rentals, sponsorships, and percentages from restaurant spending could provide the revenues to cover the financing. Without the leadership they provided, there would be no Chelsea Piers Sports Complex

The revival of Bryant Park, Herald Square, or Greeley Square would have been impossible without Daniel Biederman. Biederman was hired in 1979 to spearhead Bryant Park's reclamation. At that time, nobody knew if William H. Whyte's recommendations would work, BIDs were just emerging as a device to pay for security and sanitation along downtown shopping streets, and very few public parks were managed by nonprofit entities. Biederman saw the wisdom of and fought for combining these emerging management and financing techniques as a method for carrying out Whyte's recommendations. The energy he brought to the job provided the inspiration to overcome skeptics who wanted more information and

BIDs can be used to pay for security and sanitation in public parks managed by nonprofit entities.

Greeley Square, New York City, 2000. The 34th Street Business Improvement District has provided the capital improvements, sanitation, and security services needed to reclaim Greeley Square for active use by area workers and shoppers.

There is no reason to rollback legislation that provides incentives for property owners to create and maintain open space, and every reason to insist that this open space be accessible to the public.

further studies. Biederman coordinated designers and contractors whose specific proposals often conflicted with one another. The park that emerged should be an inspiration to all park enthusiasts.

As is clear from the success stories above, talented individuals are committed to public service. Many more are needed. One way to attract more of them is to ensure that working conditions and salaries are similar to those that are prevalent in the private sector. For that reason, we need to create institutions and jobs in which they can flourish. We also need to overcome political opposition to the high salaries that will help increase the number of true entrepreneurs attracted to public service.

A REALISTIC AGENDA

There is no reason to rollback legislation that provides incentives for property owners to create and maintain open space, and every reason to insist that this open space be accessible to the public. In urban areas, regulations must be rewritten to establish simple requirements that are easy to understand and even easier to enforce. In suburban areas, regulations should be revised so that they do not foster open space that is only available to small segments of the population. But in all instances, mandates and incentives should ensure that privately owned public open spaces are truly open to everybody.

Cities across the country have been successfully augmenting the nineteenth century open space agenda set forth by Frederick Law Olmsted. The Minneapolis Park and Recreation Board is adjusting its parks to changing market conditions. The New York City Department of Parks is implementing management techniques made possible through the use of computers. Miami Beach is repositioning its pedestrian precincts. San Francisco is reclaiming abandoned territory for public use. Boston is combining other public functions with public open space.

Their successes are based on common elements that constitute a realistic agenda for the twenty-first century. Those elements include:

- dependable, dedicated sources of financing;
- a physical plant that is in good condition;
- adequately funded, efficiently managed maintenance budgets;
- ongoing efforts to ensure that facilities provide the services their users seek;
- continual repositioning of all facilities to attract a critical mass of regular users;
- user participation in facility management that leads to advocacy for and stewardship of those facilities;
- reclaiming sites for the public realm that have been left behind by previous users; and
- attracting to public service entrepreneurial managers who will persist in their efforts to expand and enhance the public realm.

Widespread acceptance of this agenda, by its very nature and content, is dependent on a network of local constituencies. Together, these local advocates can become a political force as powerful as the coalition that implemented the Olmsted agenda. Without them, park and open space support for parks will continue to wane and financial resource will continue to dwindle.

Those communities that decide to implement this agenda should remember three of Frederick Law Olmsted's recommendations that are still as relevant as ever. First, any change or addition to the public realm, like Philadelphia's greenways, should be one that "invites, encourages, and facilitates movement," making "movement a pleasure . . . first by one promise of pleasure then by another" (Beveridge and Rocheleau 1995, 74). Second, in designing the public realm "the distinction between grounds to be used by day only, and grounds to be open night and day, needs also to be considered" (Sutton 1971, 169). Truly successful public open space, like Lincoln Road in Miami Beach, must be usable seven days a week, 52 weeks a year. Finally, the public realm should be in use long after its designers will have retired. "The people who are to visit . . . this year or next are but a small fraction of those who must be expected to visit thereafter." Thus, we must never "secure pretty temporary effects at the expense of advantages for the future" (Schuyler and Censer 1992, 539). If we follow these recommendations, we will bequeath to the next generation a public realm that is more useful, more beautiful, and more fulfilling.

List of References

Bacon, Edmund. 1998. Interview by author. 22 November.

Berens, Gayle. 1997. "Riverbank State Park.," In *Urban Parks and Open Space*, edited by Alexander Garvin and Gayle Berens. Washington, D.C.: The Urban Land Institute, 180-85.

Beveridge, Charles E. and Carolyn F. Hoffman. 1987. *The Master List of Design Projects of the Olmsted Firm, 1857-1950*. New York, N.Y.: National Association for Olmsted Parks in conjunction with the Massachusetts Association for Olmsted Parks.

Beveridge, Charles E., and Paul Rocheleau. 1995. *Frederick Law Olmsted: Designing the American Landscape*. New York: Rizzoli.

Biederman, Daniel. 1999. Interview by author. 1 June.

_____. 2001. Interview by author. 2 January.

Brambilla, Roberton, and Gianni Longo. 1977. *For Predestrians Only: Planning, Design, and Management of Traffic-free Zones*. New York: Whitney Library of Design.

Carter, Peter. 1999. *Mies Van Der Rohe at Work*. London: Phaidon Press, Ltd.

Censer, Jane Turner. ed. 1986. *The Papers of Frederick Law Olmsted*, vol. 4, *Defending the Union: The Civil War and the U.S. Sanitary Commission*, 1861-1863. Baltimore: The John Hopkins University Press.

City of New York Department of Parks and Recreation. 2000a. *Greenstreets*. New York, August.

_____. 2000b. *Parks Inspection Program Manual*. New York, New York.

Cleveland, H.W.S. 1883. "Suggestion for a System of Parks and Parkways for the City of Minneapolis." 2 June.

Fein, Albert. ed. 1968. *Landscape into Cityscape: Frederick Law Olmsted's Plans for Greater New York*. Ithaca, N.Y.: Cornell University Press.

Fox, Tom. 1990. *Urban Open Space: An Investment That Pays*. New York: The Neighborhood Open Space Coalition.

Garvin, Alexander. 1996. *The American City: What Works, What Doesn't*. New York: McGraw-Hill.

Gumprecht, Blake. 1999. *The Los Angeles River*. Baltimore, Md.: Johns Hopkins University Press.

Harnik, Peter. 1997a. "Cedar Lake Park and Trail." In *Urban Parks and Open Space*, edited by Alexander Garvin and Gayle Berens. Washington, D.C.: The Urban Land Institute, 58-69.

_____. 1997b. "Philadelphia Green." In *Urban Parks and Open Space*, edited by Alexander Garvin and Gayle Berens. Washington, D.C.: The Urban Land Institute, 158-67.

_____. 2000. *Inside City Parks*. Washington D.C.: Urban Land Institute.

Houston, Lawrence O., Jr. 1997. *Business Improvement Districts*. Washington, D.C.: The Urban Land Institute.

Kayden, Jerold S. 2000. *Privately Owned Public Space: The New York Experience*. New York: John Wiley & Sons, Inc.

Klutznick, Philip M. 1991. *Angles of Vision*. Chicago: I.R. Dee.

Morris, Marya. 2000. *Incentive Zoning: Meeting Urban Design and Affordable Housing Objectives*. Planning Advisory Service Report No. 494. Chicago: APA.

71

Moses, Robert. 1914. *The Civil Service in Great Britain.* New York: Columbia University.

National Association for Olmsted Parks. 1987. *The Master List of Design Projects of the Olmsted Firm, 1857-1950.* (Bethesda, Md.: NAOP).

New York City Citizens Housing and Planning Council. 1995. "Giuiliani Confronts *In Rem Dilemma." The Urban Prospect*, January/February.

Olmsted Brothers and Bartholomew and Associates. 1930. *Parks, Playgrounds and Beaches for the Los Angeles Region.* Reprinted in Hise, Greg, and William Deverell. 2000. *Eden by Design.* Berkeley, Calif.: University of California Press.

Olmsted, Frederick Law, Jr., and Charles Eliot. 1910. *The Improvement of Boulder Colorado.*

Olmsted, Frederick Law. 1887. *General Plan for the Improvement of the Niagara Reservation.* New York.

Ranney, Victoria Post. ed. 1990. *The Papers of Frederick Law Olmsted,* vol. 5, *The California Frontier 1863-65.* Baltimore, Md.: The John Hopkins University Press.

Reagor, Catherine. 2000. "Second Time Around." *Urban Land*, August, 107-111, 114.

Rybczynski, Witold. 1999. *A Clearing in the Distance: Frederick Law Olmsted and America in the Nineteenth Century.* (New York: Scribners).

Schuyler, David, and Jane Turner Censer. eds. 1992. *The Papers of Frederick Law Olmsted,* vol. 6, *The Years of Olmsted, Vaux and Co., 1865-1874.* Baltimore: The John Hopkins University Press.

Schwab, James C. 1992. "Urban Trees, Air Quality, and Energy Conservation." *Environment and Development*, March.

Schwanke, Dean et al. 1994. *Remaking the Shopping Center.* Washington, D.C.: The Urban Land Institute.

Sutton, S. B. ed. 1971. *Civilizing American Cities: A Selection of Frederick Law Olmsted's Writings on City Landscape.* Cambridge, Mass. The MIT Press.

Thompson, J. William. 1997. *The Rebirth of New York City's Bryant Park.* Washington, D.C., and Cambridge, Mass.: Spacemaker Press.

U.S. Bureau of the Census. 1975. *Historical Statistics of the United States: Colonial Times to 1970.* House Document No. 93-78, 93rd Congress, 1st Session.

U.S. Bureau of the Census. 1978. *Statistical Abstract of the United States: 1978.* Washington D.C.

Whyte, William H. 1980. *The Social Life of Small Urban Spaces.* New York: The Conservation Foundation.

Wirth, Theodore. 1944. *Minneapolis Park System 1883-1944.* Board of Park Commissioners of the City of Minneapolis.